CW00348854

SOFTWARE

for your

BRAIN

For a complete list of Management 2000 titles
visit our website at www.mb2000.com

SOFTWARE
for your
BRAIN

Michael Hewitt-Gleeson

2000

Copyright © Michael Hewitt-Gleeson, 1997, 2000

All rights reserved. No part of this publication may be reproduced, stored in
a retrieval system, or transmitted in any form or by any means, electronic,
mechanical, photocopying, recording, or otherwise without the prior
permission of the publishers.

Australian edition first published 1997

This new edition published 2000 by Management Books 2000 Ltd
Cowcombe House,
Cowcombe Hill,
Chalford,
Gloucestershire GL6 8HP
Tel: 01285-760722. Fax: 01285-760708

E-Mail: MB2000@compuserve.com

Printed and bound in Great Britain by Biddles, Guildford

This book is sold subject to the condition that it shall not, by way of trade
or otherwise, be lent, resold, hired out, or otherwise circulated without the
publisher's prior consent in any form of binding or cover other than that in
which it is published and without a similar condition including this
condition being imposed upon the subsequent purchaser.

The right of Michael Hewitt-Gleeson to be identified as author of this work
has been asserted by him in accordance with the Copyright, Designs and
Patents Act, 1988.

British Library Cataloguing in Publication Data is available

ISBN 1-85252-310-7

CONTENTS

Preface 7

PART 1: BRAIN VIRUS
1. Virus 13
2. PTV 16
3. Plato 20
4. PTV Software 31
5. Spread 35
6. Authority to Sovereignty 39
7. Truths 46
8. Antidote 55
Summary of Part 1 59

PART 2: BRAIN SOFTWARE
9. Software Solutions 63
10. Brainpower & Cognetics 68
11. Necktop 71
12. Start 77
13. Do 85
14. Notice 90
15. Think 100
16. CVS ≠ BVS 111
17. BVS = CVS x 10 121
18. Tenpower 125
19. CVSTOBVS 131
20. Quality 143
21. Recognition 148
22. Humour 155
23. Practice 165
24. Repetition 170
25. Rehearsal 176
26. ICD 183
Summary of Part 2 191

To Dad. From a grateful son.

To Galileo. From a grateful sun.

PREFACE

I HAVE ALWAYS thought of my country, Australia, as a clever country. We even export cleverness! Australia continues to grow and export some of the world's best scientists. Indeed, the School of Thinking (SOT) based in Melbourne and also in Cyberia (on the Internet at www.sot.com.au), is now the largest school in the world, daily exporting thinking lessons to every country on the planet.

There are more scientists alive today than all the scientists who ever lived. In every sphere of knowledge, these scientists are questioning, exploring, experimenting, researching and updating what we once thought to be true.

As a scientist, I was taught that old truths are replaced by new truths as new evidence becomes available. As a human being living in today's world I don't need to be a scientist to realise this obvious fact.

The world is full of daily examples of this phenomenon – the explosion of knowledge, the information revolution, the high-tech advances in Cybermedia, the sophistication of the marketplace, productivity increases in the workplace, the changes in geopolitical spheres of influence, and the way in which sporting records continue to be shattered.

Replacing old truths is called *thinking*. To help promote this activity, I started the School of Thinking (SOT) in New York in 1979. SOT lessons have now reached over 50 million people worldwide. In a USAir article, SOT was once described as the 'McDonald's of thinking'.

I have sometimes been accused by the intellectual elite of 'selling thinking to the masses'. I take it as a compliment, since I cannot think of a better thing to sell. SOT, now the largest school in the world, teaches not what to think but HOW to think – thinking as a skill – and provides daily thinking lessons to anyone, any place, any time.

SOT's mission has always been to get 'thinking' taught to kids at

7

school by placing 'thinking' on the curriculum as a school subject. At first, there was quite a lot of resistance to this proposal. But it did receive wonderful support from some very special people, like my mentor, Professor George Gallup (founder of the Gallup Poll at Princeton), who once encouraged me by telling me, 'I believe your work in teaching people to think may be the most important thing going on in the world today.'

Eventually, after ten years of running around the US from New York to places like Washington, Dallas, San Francisco, Puerto Rico, etc., and back to New York again, talking to parents, teachers, legislators, the media, business and others, we met with great success.

In the mid-eighties, 'teaching thinking' became a nationwide fad in US education led by media articles in two of America's most influential publications – a cover story I gave to Readers Digest; and a lead article about our project in the New York Times, 'Teaching Thinking: A New Emphasis at Schools and Colleges' (9 January 1983).

On returning to Australia in the bi-centennial year of 1988, I launched the School of Thinking at a meeting of 700 of Australia's municipal and federal statespeople in Canberra. To commemorate the occasion, I presented the Governor-General, His Excellency Sir Ninian Stephen AK, GCMB, GCVO, KBE, with his own SOT Brainusers Kit and then awarded to the Hon. Robert J. L. Hawke AK, the Prime Minister of Australia and a former Rhodes Scholar, a special certificate appointing him as 'Australia's Number One Brainuser'. Prime Minister Hawke decreed: 'No longer content to be just the lucky country, Australia must now become the clever country.'

Since bringing the SOT to Australia, I have worked a similar campaign to the one I used in the US, touring Australia giving lectures and working the media to see that Australian kids are taught to think for themselves. The better way to do this is to have 'thinking' put on the core curriculum as a school subject Then kids will learn that knowing HOW to think is every bit as important as knowing what to think.

In 1995, the House of Representatives Standing Committee on Industry, Science and Technology invited the School of Thinking to advise on how Australia can further develop its 'innovation culture'. Part of our submission to the Parliament said as follows:-

'Developing an innovation culture in Australia is the greatest strategic hope for our productive future in this economic region. The biggest obstacle we face in doing this is the cultural lack of value we place on 'thinking and innovation' compared to the value we place on being 'right' and defending our point-of-view.

'This is historically due to the importation of our education system from Europe. Since the Church designed our European education system in the Middle Ages, the traditional focus of education has been on teaching children what to think. To date, we have not had an equal balance given to teaching our children how to think. Generally, this has tended to produce culture which, like other European cultures, feels it is more important to be 'right' than to be a thinker, to experiment, to make mistakes, to discover, to take risks... to innovate!

'The mission of the School of Thinking is also to see that thinking is taught in Australian schools as a core curriculum subject, by 1999.

'Today everyone is talking about the human brain. It's the new frontier. In the increasingly competitive global business theatre, world class corporations are realising that the cleverness of their employees – their brainpower – is the ultimate corporate asset. There is a new trend towards developing, managing and measuring the 'intellectual capital' of the corporate enterprise. As a senior IBM executive said, 'Our most valuable corporate assets go home at 5pm and are not even recorded on the balance sheet'.

'The School of Thinking believes the most successful and secure route to an 'innovation culture' or a 'clever country' is TO PUT THINKING AS A SKILL ON THE CORE CURRICULUM OF THE EDUCATION SYSTEM.

'If a child goes to school for ten or more years and never has a thinking lesson, that child can be forgiven for getting the impression that thinking is not as important as knowing things.

They feel that being 'right' and defending one's own viewpoint is more important than escaping from one's viewpoint to find an even better one – the cognitive process we call innovation.

'On the other hand, if a child receives deliberate training in thinking skills, if 'thinking' has a place on the curriculum, then that child sees a value being placed on 'thinking'. That society has shown it values thinking and has positioned itself as having an innovation culture.'

(Extract from) Submission to the House of Representatives Standing Committee on Industry, Science and Technology regarding the Committee's inquiry into innovation in Australia, by Dr Michael Hewitt-Gleeson, Founder & Principal of the School of Thinking 1 February, 1995.

As a result, it has now become government policy to introduce 'teaching thinking' into all schools and teacher colleges in Australia and Territories (see Parliament of Commonwealth of Australia - Standing Committee Report on Innovation, November 1995).

It is a very hopeful thing that future Australian kids will be taught not just to get the 'right' answers and to defend 'The Truth', but also how to find *new truths* and to think for themselves.

Anyway, enough of the drum-beating and on with the show.....

Michael Hewitt-Gleeson
Melbourne

Part I

BRAIN VIRUS

1

VIRUS

What if you had a virus in your brain? What if it was a cognitive virus, a kind of cognitive AIDS? What would it do to you? How would it affect your thinking? How did you get infected with the virus? What could you do to cure it?

EVERY TECHNOLOGY has its hackers – enthusiasts who enjoy exploring the intimate details of the system, cracking the codes and stretching and testing the capabilities of systems. There have been radio hackers and CB hackers and you've no doubt read about the telephone hackers who have ripped-off the phone companies for millions of pounds in free long-distance calls.

We've seen nuclear hackers who have designed DIY nuclear weapons for science projects and today we have computer hackers who roam the networks for fun and profit. No doubt it won't be long before we read of genetic hackers who amuse themselves by playing around in our gene pool. Hackers, driven by strong curiosity, often just start off by seeking amusement and showing off their skill but sometimes their antics lead to chaos, fraud and even... disaster!

In recent years, some computer hackers started out manipulating their systems for fun by designing viruses that replicate themselves into other systems. Few hackers, however, are competent enough or even willing to fully comprehend the ongoing consequences of their antics.

Many of their viruses took off out of control and by now have infected millions of personal computers. These viruses are real! They cause real downtime, real loss of capital, real damage to equipment, real destruction of databases – and, sometimes, real loss of life.

Donald Latham of Computer Sciences Corporation and a former White House Assistant Secretary of Defence, says, 'The dangers of viruses are just unbelievable – the threat is more serious than most people think.'

Daily cybertransactions that can be infected by computer viruses include:-

- Wall Street decisions involving the transfer of capital in the £billions.
- Credit-card transactions between millions of traders and their customers.
- Airline reservations affecting thousands of travellers.
- Maintenance and command decisions involving hundreds of US missiles and others.

The mind boggles at the havoc that can be caused if these viruses spread unchecked. Yet there is a virus, a brain virus, which already exists in the brains of many humans from preachers to presidents, that makes these computer viruses look wimps by comparison. This brain virus is real. It's seductive and it's very powerful. It's also highly destructive and has been fatal to over 200 million humans JUST THIS CENTURY. In the brain of a president it could unleash a missile that starts the unthinkable nuclear madness that threatens the very existence of humanity. In the brain of a CEO it can threaten the survival of the business.

And in YOUR brain???

This brain virus is the Plato Truth Virus and the chances are almost certain that you, dear brainuser, are already infected. In Part One of this book you will come to understand the virus and how it affects your life, and in Part Two you will find out exactly what you can do to contain it.

Plato the hacker

When it comes to 'thinking', Plato was the ultimate hacker.

At that time, playing around with thinking systems was as much the rage amongst an elite group of men in Greece, as playing around with software systems is the rage amongst the hackers of today. Socrates, Plato and Aristotle were the most famous 'thinking hackers' of their day. These hackers of 2,500 years ago designed fundamental thinking technologies; systems and viruses that have dominated Western thinking right up to now, and who knows for how much longer?

Today's hackers have handles like AcidFreak and CyberSam. Plato's handle could well have been TruthFreak since it was he who invented his 'truth' concept – the strange notion that there is such a thing as 'objective truth'.

Yet this bizarre suggestion has so side-tracked Western philosophers that even today many great minds in Western colleges and universities have still not escaped from Plato's 'truth' idea and their thinking remains infected with this dangerous virus.

It would be a difficult (but worthwhile) project to calculate the cost to humanity and the staggering destruction caused by Plato's 'truth' virus. It's unlikely that Plato had any idea of the extreme consequences of his invention any more than some of today's hackers will have of theirs. He was just hacking around with thinking.

In the next few chapters we'll take a careful look at the Plato Truth Virus: What is it? How does it work? What does it do? What is the up side and down side of the virus? How did the virus become so virulent? Who spread it around? How did you become infected? What is it doing to your brain? Is there a cure?

2

PTV

IN PART ONE of this book we will be dealing head-on with the biggest obstacle that may prevent you being an effective thinker. It's also the biggest cognitive restriction stopping you developing your intellectual capital.

It's called PTV or the Plato Truth Virus.

Cognitive dissonance

In cognitive science, the term 'cognitive dissonance' is often used. Cognitive dissonance is interesting because it refers to what happens in your brain when information is presented to it which doesn't seem to fit.

For example, just suppose the current state of information in your brain was such that you believed the earth was flat. This of course, seems naive to us now but not long ago most smart people saw things this way. Now, suppose someone called Fred comes along and says, 'No, the earth is round!' and tries to explain to you why you should change your view. You would begin to experience cognitive dissonance. If, though you thought the earth was flat, you were not superstitiously committed to that view you might only experience a mild case of cognitive dissonance. Then, as you followed the evidence Fred presented, you might find your view evolving from 'flat earth' to 'round earth'.

If, on the other hand, you not only believed the earth was flat but you also believed your 'flat earth' view was 'absolutely right', then you might have a dose of strong cognitive dissonance, so strong that it might be easier to burn Fred at the stake than to change your view from 'flat earth' to 'round earth'.

The father of modern science

This kind of thing is not just a silly story but actually does happen. One of the most notorious examples was that of the Father of Modern Science, the brilliant 17th century mathematician, Galilei Galileo.

Galileo had constructed his telescope to show how the earth revolved about the sun and not the sun around the earth. Since Copernicus first advanced this hypothesis it had caused great controversy. Galileo now had proof.

When he demonstrated this, many highly intelligent people refused even to look through the telescope, so frightened were they of what they might see. Some people had such a strong dose of cognitive dissonance that they forced Galileo to his knees and made him withdraw his evidence and recant his discovery.

In 1633, Galileo, 70 years old, sick and completely blind, was forced by the Pope to make the arduous journey to Rome to stand trial for 'heresy'. Urban VIII, taking time off from cannibalising the Colosseum to build his Barberini palace, accused Galileo of causing 'the greatest scandal in Christendom' for contradicting the Scriptures.

Galileo thought of himself as a devoted Catholic. He argued that the bible was not a scientific text and that we should not expect its 'scientific statements' to be taken literally. He argued that it presents no challenge to faith; that both nature and the bible are divine texts and cannot contradict one another.

On 21 June, after a long trial, he was found guilty of heresy by the Inquisition. Not only that, he was bullied and actually forced into covering up his evidence. The Pope demanded that he be tortured if he did not obey:-

'The said Galileo is in the judgement of the Holy Office vehemently suspected of heresy, namely, of having believed

*and held the doctrine which is false and contrary to the Sacred
and Divine Scriptures that the sun is the centre of the world and
does not move from east to west, and is not the centre of the
world.'*

Weary and broken, the old man knelt before the Pope and made his
confession:-

'I, Galileo, son of the late Vincenzo Galilei, Florentine, aged
seventy years... must altogether abandon the false opinion that
the sun is the centre of the world and immobile'.

His trial was a grave and solemn milestone in the history of the
Church only surpassed in poignancy by the trial of Jesus before Pilate.
Galileo was a brilliant mathematician and a pioneer of science which,
of course, does not rely on dogma. He advocated the idea that 'The
Book of Nature' is written in mathematical characters, a view which
in itself is enough to make him a founding father of the scientific
method.

The universe which Galileo observed at the end of his telescope
totally dwarfed the one that people were seeing with their ordinary
vision. He tried to show that it was important to consider the value of
new observable phenomena as a way of escaping from weak truths
and moving to better ones.

The superstitious, ecclesiastical, Roman brainusers of the 17th
century experienced such cognitive dissonance from Galileo's
discoveries that, to their everlasting shame, they chose to abuse and
bully an old man rather than to change their own minds.

The cognitive dissonance endured so strongly that it was only in
1993 (after a 12-year Pontifical Commission!) that, in a belated burst
of Christian charity, the Vatican brainusers finally 'forgave' Galileo
for letting the sun out of the closet. Better late than never, I suppose.

Dosage of dissonance

It may be that some of the material in this book gives you a certain amount of cognitive dissonance. It is difficult to design the ideal dosage of dissonance. What is fine for some readers and is just enough to help them to open up their mind will, on the other hand, be too strong for others and cause them to close down.

For example, earlier drafts of this book were more provocative in tone and probably too much so. So I sought the opinions of a fairly wide range of brainusers – different ages, different cultures, different professions, different backgrounds.

After receiving the generous and valuable feedback of hundreds of readers (especially that of my father who is the fairest man I have ever met) I completely rewrote the book and tried to find a better balance between the information I have left in and the information I have left out. Thanks to them it's a better book but the faults you may find are still mine.

At the end of the day, dear brainuser, my own goal for this book has always been to generate enough cognitive dissonance to make it interesting reading but not so much as to close your mind.

3

PLATO

PLATO'S ORIGINAL idea was that there is such a thing as objective, 'absolute truth'. Plato's 'truth' idea (like all his ideas) was a product of his imagination.

He was the younger friend of Socrates whom he admired greatly and who was also his mentor. It was Socrates who invented the interrogatory style of argument involving strings of questions seeking either a YES or NO response. It's the old dinosaur known as the Socratic Method but it still survives in our legal system and can still be seen on TV shows like LA Law and the O. J. Simpson trial.

Both Socrates and Plato became two of the greatest thinking hackers in Western history. To me, the most fascinating of Plato's works is the Symposium because it's an insightful account of how it all began at a typical dinner-party back in Athens around 400 BC, with Plato, Socrates and a few friends.

It's witty, entertaining and shows how their discussions and banter, laced with much wine and bawdy gossip, produced a small collection of thinking ploys, concepts, software and viruses that, amazingly, have dominated Western thinking right up to the 21st century.

Most destructive of all these inventions has been the Plato Truth Virus.

In the Western world, Plato is recognised as the one who put thinking on the map. Plato figured that the more one thought about matters and the more one tried to discover and understand their true essence or form, the more insights one could experience. But he also decided (and this is the killer) that thinking was NOT an open-ended process. Plato figured there must be a finite end to a thinker's relentless search for meaning, an ultimate destination to a thinker's efforts, so he called that destination objective 'truth'. Uh-oh! Big mistake!!

Today, 2,500 years later, much of Western society still behaves as though there actually is such a thing as an objective, absolute truth. Somehow oblivious to real world consequences, many Western universities and colleges are full of discussions about 'truth', 'right', 'wrong', 'good', 'evil', 'honesty', 'justice' and so on. This all spills out into society so that Big Government, Big Religion, Big Business, Big Brother and other (smaller) groups invoke these 'absolute truths' as the basis for their policies and the justification for their actions – so often with horrific consequences.

The trouble was that once Plato had invented his truth concept, it existed. Subsequently, when other thinkers came along, Plato's invention infected their ideas like a virus – and so we name the virus after him, the Plato Truth Virus (PTV). Gradually, the activity of thinking came to be subverted by the insidious truth virus. Some thinkers inevitably claimed to have found – The Truth.

PTV, the truth virus, began to control the thinkers' set of intellectual claims and so we see a number of philosophies and doctrines and movements that claimed to have discovered absolute truth and gave notice of filing their claims. 'Stop looking! ... We have the truth! ... We are right, you are wrong! ... We are good, you are evil! ... Believe in the truth or be damned! ... The truth is on our side! ... We know what's right! Do what we tell you, or else! Crush the infidel!- Kill the unbeliever!'

My-teacher-is-right-your-teacher-is-wrong!

The problem for the observer is the number of conflicting claims to absolute truth and unique rightness. The seductiveness of PTV is also what makes it so destructive and deadly: everyone wants to be the one who has 'The Truth'. Therefore, everyone infected with the virus claims to be uniquely right and that's where the carnage begins.

From time to time, teachers like Buddha, Jesus and Confucius have emerged in the different cultures of the world. More people are free of PTV and many have benefited from their teachers' messages of goodwill.

Sadly, these teachers are often upstaged by greedy, PTV-infected franchisees who claim to have exclusive rights on their teacher's intellectual property. Who can blame the original teachers for the sickness of their followers?

So often, in the name of peace and goodwill, infected followers fight with a sick rage and burning hatred. The brain virus so distorts the original message that it would be unrecognisable to the original messenger. People have become more interested in the 'truth status' of the message than the message itself. Perhaps it is more important to be an 'effective follower' than to be a 'right follower'.

Truths 'R' Us

Here is a small sample of PTV-infected claims which have long since upstaged those claims made by the original teacher:-

Christian Science:

...is unerring and Divine... outside of Christian Science all is vague and hypothetical, the opposite of Truth.

Seventh-Day Adventists:

The General Conference of Seventh-Day Adventists is the highest authority that God has upon earth.

Jehovah's Witnesses:

...alone are God's true people, and all others without exception are followers of the Devil... At Armageddon all of earth's inhabitants except Jehovah's Witnesses will be wiped out of existence.

Mormons:

There is no salvation outside the Church of Jesus Christ of Latter-Day Saints... everybody, unless they repent and work righteousness, will be damned except Mormons.

Christadelphians:

None but Christadelphians can be saved.

Islam:

Mohammed is the messenger of God... the last, and final exponent of God's mind, the seal of the prophets.

The Divine Light Mission:

The Guru Marahaji alone has the key to the knowledge of the source of God.

The Unification Church (moonies):

Only the Lord of the Second Advent, the Reverend Sun Myung Moon, will be powerful enough to complete the restoration of man to God.

Krishna Consciousness:

Direct love for the Lord Krishna, in the form of chanting, singing and dancing, is the best way to rid the soul of ignorance.

Church of Scientology:

It is only through the exercise of the principles of Dianetics that there is real hope for happiness in this lifetime and the eventual freeing of the soul from death.

The Children of God:

No power in the world can stand against the power of David. (This refers to David Berg, the sect's leader.)

Catholic Church:

No one can be saved without that faith which the Holy, Catholic, Apostolic, Roman Church holds, believes and teaches... the One True Church established on earth by Jesus Christ... to whom alone it belongs to judge the meaning and interpretation of the Holy Scriptures.

In spite of these corporate claims and the consequences they have caused to millions, most members of these groups are not infected with PTV. Most of the faithful are people of genuine peace who quietly go about their business. They try to live by their creeds without bothering others at all. The silent majority are not the villains.

If there were ever such a thing as 'absolute truth', by its own definition, there could only be one 'absolute truth'. So, which truth is the true truth?

As a philosophical piece of gamesmanship, this coveting of the label of absolute truth is not limited to religious doctrines, but spills over into political, business, sociological, and even economic theories, although the latter have fallen on hard times lately.

At first, adding the label of 'absolute truth' seemed to make a set of intellectual claims or doctrines superior to those that were not absolute, but time has shown the opposite to be the case. We know now that once the thinking effort switches to defence and support (as it must if a doctrine is frozen as absolute truth), further growth and creative development are discouraged. The truth begins to lose its credibility as it begins to lose its relevance and its effectiveness. 'The Truth' inevitably serves to undermine the doctrine it was originally meant to reinforce.

Two people can, of course, have two different points of view. Nothing odd about that. But, if each viewpoint is infected with PTV, if each believes his viewpoint is 'uniquely right', PTV can keep them fighting and bullying each other for some time.

Replace two people with two families, two communities, two groups, two religions or two nations and this pernicious truth virus can be passed on to each successive generation and the fighting and persecution continue for hundreds of years.

It may be that Plato's truth virus has done more damage to human society than any human thinking device ever invented. Just this past century alone more than 100 million humans have been killed by PTV and the process shows no sign of stopping.

Myths, theories and hypotheses

It does seem to be a genuine, legitimate and universal need of the human mind to create myths, stories, theories and hypotheses to explain and make coherent an unexplainable world.

Example:

When frightened by a thunderstorm some thinkers explained it as a burst of Zeus' anger. Others later said it was an electrostatic phenomenon. An illness can be seen by some as a voodoo spell or by others as a viral infection. In an attempt to perform their function of making sense out of chaos, myths and scientific theories work on the same principle. The view that we humans build of our world is always a product of our imagination.

Your view of a situation is a cognitive phenomenon. In a situation, your experience of the situation is an electrochemical event which takes place in your brain. The phrase 'your experience of the situation' is important because it points to the uniqueness of your understanding of the situation. Others in the situation will also have their own unique experience of it. Which is right?

Example:

I love movies. I am a regular movie-goer. I find movies to be great value. In movies, hundreds of talented people spend thousands of hours and millions of dollars to create a product that I can enjoy for £5. Where else do you get such enormous leverage of value? When I tell you about a recent movie I have seen, am I telling you about the movie, or, am I telling you about my experience of the movie? When a movie critic writes about a movie, is she writing about the movie, or is she writing about her understanding of the movie? Note the distinction.

There is a distinction and it is a crucial one. PTV is a problem because it can distort the host brain's ability to make the distinction. The virus-impaired brain may be unable to distinguish between its parochial experience and that of other brains. The PTV brain thinks its experience is uniquely right.

Bores and bullies

The sick brain can cause people to become bores or bullies, I'm not sure which is worse.

The boring brainuser is one whose behaviour is wearying others because he or she cannot stop their tedious, enthusiastic talk about their own interests and experience, not because others are interested but because PTV makes them assume others are interested. Many companies train their salespeople to become bores who annoy their prospects and prevent them from ever becoming customers.

It would be interesting to measure the profits lost to shareholders who have no idea what they are losing due to management's archaic, PTV-infected sales doctrines.

PTV can wreck a business. It can cause brainusers automatically to assume that other brainusers are aligned to their unique interests or products when they are so unlikely to be.

Or, PTV can cause a brainuser to need, want, or demand others to share their 'uniquely right' experience of a situation. The infected brain can cause behaviour that employs pressure, coercion or even force to frighten or bully other brainusers to toe the line.

So much time, effort, peace and productivity have been wasted by nagging bores and tiresome bullies.

Yes, the human brain is an explanation-manufacturing mechanism but that's not the same thing as explaining. Do notice the difference. By creating explanations to fill in the gaps when needed, the brain helps to keep us mentally stable. This will always be a useful property of the human brain.

Thinking, being a thinker, having a healthy curiosity is a normal part of the functioning of a healthy human brain. What is not healthy or normal but is a very dangerous cognitive disease is the condition of the 'true believer'. In pop psychology terms, thinkers are OK but true believers are NOT OK.

The symptom of the true believer is the colloquial and very crippled viewpoint that says, 'I have the truth'... 'My policy is the true policy'... 'My doctrine is good and your doctrine is evil'... or, perhaps, 'Wasn't I lucky to be born into that True Religion and now what are we going to do about you, unbeliever?' It is difficult to imagine a more dangerous mental condition.

In the preface of his book, *The True Believers* (Methuen 1986) Peter Bowler warns:

'Here they come, the True Believers, wide-eyed and earnest; here they come, the devotees, the fanatics, the evangelists, the pilgrims, the worshippers, the contemplatives – clutching their hymns and invocations, observing their holy commandments and taboos, performing their sacrifices but, above all – believing. Believing in God, or in several gods, or even a goddess or two. Believing in the soul, in demons, in eternal forgiveness, in eternal punishment, in life after death, in assorted varieties of heaven and hell, in the power of faith to heal, to move mountains...

'They are and always have been, the idealists of humankind. Seeking something beyond the material something intangible, something to explain the unexplainable, something to assuage their fear of the uncontrollable, something to compensate them for the unacceptable, something to offer them a kind of dignity and power in the midst of indignity and impotence. Let us not mock the True Believer for their idealism. But watch out for them – they can be dangerous. Combative people, they are, by nature; crusaders rather than compromisers. Because they are right, others are wrong; the sinful must be punished, and who more sinful than the unbeliever? The more intolerant and warlike among them seek to punish the unbeliever in this life, with holy wars and Inquisitions; the more benevolent and tolerant leave it to their God to punish the unbeliever with eternal torments after death.

'From time to time history has thrown up a sect that is gentle and moderate and peace loving, like the Quakers or the Baha'i; invariably these sects are singled out for the most ruthless persecution at the hands of the True Believers.

'When two religions are so similar as to be almost identical in every significant respect then take cover, because the conflict between them will be truly murderous. Buddhists and Presbyterians get along famously, but if you are selling insurance you would be ill-advised to set up shop in Palestine or Belfast.'

For example, in the Middle Ages, the number of Europeans who died or were killed as a result of the Crusades is put at approximately four million. The victims of the Inquisition in Spain alone, included:

* 30,000 burned at the stake
* 17,000 burned in effigy
* 290,000 punished by torture, prison or financial ruin.

Of all these victims, most were women, 'heretics' and Jews.

Today?

That's all very sad, of course, but those medieval days are gone now, aren't they? Today we live in the Age of Aquarius and as we approach the new millennium, isn't all that truth virus stuff rather old hat and even slightly alarmist to us cool, laid-back dudes? 'Fraid not...! For example, recent world's headlines were filled with stories about a group in Japan whose ideas are very much infected with the truth virus. Time magazine's cover story (3 April 1995) was about a group that poisoned 3,000 Tokyo subway commuters with nerve gas. Time reported:-

'In what could only have been a carefully co-ordinated, painstakingly planned atrocity, an apparently diluted form of nerve gas called sarin, a weapon of mass killing originally concocted by the Nazis, was placed simultaneously in five subway cars at morning rush hour, killing 10 victims and sickening thousands more... (later at the suspect group's compound) policemen in protective suits with canaries emerged with ton after ton of chemicals – sodium cyanide, sodium fluoride, phosphorus trichloride, isopropyl alcohol, acetonitrile... enough to kill 4.2 million people.'

Later, it was reported that police found containers of a biological toxin called botulinum, one of the world's deadliest germs. They found enough to wipe out the whole planet! Presumably this would be justifiable, all in the name of truth. As a result of this atrocity, 'The Japanese have lost their trust in society,' says sociologist Kenichi Tominaga of Keio University. 'It will never be the same.'

And the name of this post-modern group of the 1990s? Aum Shinrikyo which means – SUPREME TRUTH!

PTV is not just a medieval curiosity. Today, PTV is still very much alive and may be living it up in your brain! Listen!

Thought experiment

Sit quietly now for about three to five minutes and notice the activity going on in your brain. Try to notice the thought patterns, the dissonance, the defences that PTV is working to preserve its survival. What have you noticed about your thinking patterns and what, if anything, have you noticed about PTV's activities in your brain?

4

PTV SOFTWARE

IF PLATO WAS the hacker who invented the truth virus, Aristotle was the first to package it into a powerful cognitive operating system or thinking software package.

Aristotle started as a student in Plato's academy and remained there for 20 years until Plato, his mentor, died. By the time Plato died Aristotle was thoroughly infected with his mentor' truth virus and did much to establish 'the search for certainty as the basis of all intellectual endeavours.'

Aristotle became a passionate and obsessive truth freak. Plato only went as far as saying that truth was what lay at the long end of a thinker's search, an ultimate destination. Not enough for Ari ... No sir! Aristotle said, 'I want truth! I want it here! I want it now!'

Aristotle went on to insist that the ordinary fuzzy jumble of our daily reality was just not tidy enough. So, to bring order to the world he imposed a kind of truth template over everything.

Mail-sorting and labelling

Aristotle's medium was language. He assumed that the certainty of words could give certainty to the ineffable flow of experience. The untidy chaos of reality offended Aristotle's ordered, PTV-infected mind so he decided to break everything up into pigeonholes and categories – kind of like mail-sorting and labelling.

This goes here, that goes there, stick this label on this and that label on that! Let's just tidy everything up. Yessir. A place for everything and everything in its place was Aristotle's motto.

In his classifying fervour Aristotle made up pigeonholes and sorted our daily reality into them. He tried to invent slots for everything. For example, he set about sorting 'government' into categories like:-

'constitutional', 'tyrannical', 'monarchy', 'aristocracy', 'oligarchy', 'democracy'.

He then got busy breaking everything up into subjects, like:-

'politics', 'ethics', 'rhetoric' (speech-making), 'metaphysics', 'physics', 'biology', 'meteorology'.

Finally, he invented his very own thinking software called 'logic'.

Aristotle's silly syllogism

Aristotle's thinking software was already infected with the Plato Truth Virus from day one. For logic, Aristotle invented his silly syllogism. I say it's silly because it lacks wisdom and sense.

The syllogism starts with the so-called 'truth' as its premise. Then one simply matches up items that come along and out pops your conclusion. Simple really... and very silly.

Examples:

TRUTH:	ITEM:
All swans are white.	This is a swan.
LOGICAL EXTENSION:	Therefore it is white.
TRUTH:	ITEM:
Salespeople tell lies.	Amy is a salesperson.
LOGICAL CONCLUSION:	Therefore Amy is lying.
TRUTH:	ITEM:
Our church is the right church.	You are not a member.
LOGICAL CONCLUSION:	Therefore you are wrong.

TRUTH:	ITEM:
The earth is flat.	Therefore it has an edge.
LOGICAL CONCLUSION:	Therefore you will fall off the edge if you go too far.

TRUTH:	ITEM:
The President is the law.	The President did something.
LOGICAL CONCLUSION:	Therefore it is legal.

(Aristotle's Logic software caused Nixon to believe this.)

TRUTH:	ITEM:
A boss's opinion is best.	You are not a boss.
LOGICAL CONCLUSION:	So when we want your opinion we'll give it to you...

No contradictions, please!

For Aristotle, just thinking wasn't good enough. No, you have to think logically. Logic is obsessed with hunting down contradictions. In logic, a thing cannot be in box 'A' and box 'NOT A' at the same time. No, it must be sorted and classified into the 'correct' box.

Although real life is full of contradictions and paradoxes (is the glass half full or half empty?) this was just not good enough for our man Aristotle. Things must be cut up into pieces like a jig-saw and then sorted into their 'true' categories.

Judging right from wrong

Life, according to Aristotle, is a matter of sorting things out into 'right' and 'wrong'. Judgement is the key activity. This is right. That's wrong. I'm right. You're wrong. This is black. That is white. This is American. That's un-American. This is good. That is bad. This is the right answer. That is the wrong answer.

Greyness? Fuzziness? Uncertainty? Open-endedness? Paradox?

Contradiction? Well, we cannot have that sort of thing around here. You've got to sort things out! Clean up your act! Get things right! In Aristotle's Lyceum, everything was covered by rules, rules, rules. The living arrangements, the study courses, the timetables were all dominated by rules and regulations.

Ancient software

Aristotle craved order. He loved the order that his classifications brought to his ideas and thoughts. He assumed that the same order that he found he could impose on words and language could also be imposed on the real world. Many have made the same mistake.

Aristotle's cognitive operating system, logic, has dominated Western education for far too long. How come we still think this way 2,500 years after old Ari joined Socrates and Plato on Mount Olympus? How come this ancient software has survived so long? Who kept it alive? Who spread it around? Who programmed it into your brain? We will discuss this in the next chapter.

Thought experiment

Have a look around. Try to notice Aristotle's PTV-infected logic software in operation. You should try to notice it in your own mental information-processing and also in that of others. Look for it in this book. Look for evidence of the virus in today's newspaper and on TV. Also, try to notice it in institutions and in common situations you come across in the next 24 hours. It is so pervasive that you may have difficulty noticing the very subtle manifestations.

5

SPREAD

IN THE LAST FEW chapters we looked at PTV, the Plato Truth Virus. We saw how the 'thinking' hackers of ancient Athens – Socrates, Plato and Aristotle – fooled around with 'thinking' software and how they developed and packaged the concept of 'absolute truth'.

In these next few chapters we'll explore how PTV was picked up and spread throughout the Western world, infecting millions of minds and killing millions of human beings and is still flourishing 2,500 years later.

In tracking the spread of a virus, we can try to find our way back to the identification of its Patient Zero. Who was the first patient who really got the virus going? Who was the one to spread it around enough to let it take hold?

Well, when it came to the spreading of Aristotle's Logi Software (already infected with PTV) no-one was more successful than a young Italian nobleman, Thomas Aquinas.

'Doctor Truth' and the truth

Born in 1225 into powerful nobility near Naples, Aquinas outraged his family when he decided to become a Dominican friar. When it comes to truth freaks, Thomas was one of the greatest ever. He was Doctor Truth himself!

Thomas discovered a new translation of Aristotle from the Greek and so he set out to synthesise Aristotelian ideas in such a way that it was useful for defending The Truth.

Of course, as far as The Truth was concerned, there was never any doubt for our Fra Thomas. No need to look around. No need to search. He already knew exactly where and exactly what The Truth was. There was no further search required for The Truth as far as Aquinas was concerned. Just a matter of defending it and preserving it from any attempt to change it.

The Truth, proclaimed Thomas, was the teachings of the Church. And whose church might that be, Thomas? The Muslims? The Buddhists? The Jews? Picture Thomas opening the envelope, 'And the winner is ... The Catholic Church!'

That's it! Nothing else. Stop looking. Here it is. The lucky winner! Well, now, the winning True Church also happens to be YOUR church, Thomas old chap. What a coincidence! What a stroke of luck!

As it happened, Thomas' Church was the Microsoft of its time, an information monopoly. All European universities were run by the Church with head office in Rome. Rome literally owned all of knowledge and was busily exporting its corporate education system. The powerful but flawed thinking software, logic, was the cognitive operating system they used, courtesy of Aristotle via Aquinas.

This educational enterprise amounted to programming brains with what the church taught – verbatim – and repeating it back again. Scholarship was reduced to mere defence of Vatican teachings, which were known collectively as – The Truth.

Only Microsoft's export of Bill Gates' DOS – and later, Windows – has ever rivalled the Vatican's export of Thomas Aquinas' PTV.

Today, there are around 350 million PC users in the world and when they turn on their desktop or laptop computer the first thing over 300 million of them see is the word 'Windows'. This is an amazing accomplishment for Bill Gates and Microsoft in less than 20 years. This is only beaten by the fact that all 350 million PC users are also necktop users. And all 350 million are using Vatican-exported logic operating system to work their necktop computers so they can work their PCs!

In the original Thomist Aristotle neuroware, the logic operating system worked like this:

TRUTH:	Vatican teaching is The Truth.
ITEM:	Using Aristotle's logic to match things up, we are meant to ask: Does ITEM match TRUTH?
LOGICAL CONCLUSION:	If YES, then it is RIGHT and it is TRUTH. If NO, then it is WRONG and is HERESY.

Even people with the most superficial knowledge of history know what happened to heretics.

Truth machines

I was recently in Amsterdam and paid a visit to the notorious Inquisition's Torture Museum. This popular tourist spot features a collection of 'truth machines', an extraordinary array of macabre machines, racks, tongs, and spikes.

These and other implements of torture were used by the Inquisitors to 'purify' the heretics. One could only marvel uneasily at the cold-blooded ingenuity that went into the design of these instruments of truth.

The Inquisitors, invariably, were Fra Thomas's fellow Dominicans. They were quite willing to inflict unspeakable horrors on thousands upon thousands of fellow human beings just for disagreeing. Thomist Aristotle doctrine could show up any contradictions.

It could show that their point-of-view did not exactly match The Truth, and so they were heretics. Cut out their tongues! Crank up the rack! Get me the branding iron! Off to the stake! It still sends shivers down my spine.

Angelic 'Doctor Truth'...

In the 14th century, the 'Angelic Doctor' was canonised for his great contribution to the defence of truth and Saint Thomas Aquinas became a kind of god in the church. There even is a famous painting by Zurbaran called 'The Apotheosis of St Thomas Aquinas' which shows Thomas, resplendent on a cloud in heaven in those frightening Dominican Inquisitorial robes, with popes and scholars at his feet. And below on earth, other popes and cardinals look up and pray to him in admiration.

John XXII said that to deny Aquinas was tantamount to heresy. Later, in 1879, Pope Leo XIII proclaimed that Thomist Aristotelian doctrine should be accepted as 'the official doctrine of the church'.

Exporting the virus

Since Aquinas imbedded Aristotle's logic into the Vatican's education system it has become the main thinking software of Western civilisation, wherever it has been exported.

Since then, The Truth has been carried to all parts of the world with missionary zeal. In fact, Western education may be medieval Europe's most successful export.

Australia is a good example. Although Australia is geographically in South East Asia, it has culturally been in Europe for the past 200 years. At that time, along with rabbits, the Western education system was imported into Australia.

Since World War II, however, Australia has become less Eurocentric and more Euro-Asian. Australia is now one of the world's most successful multi-cultural societies. Accordingly, 'unique rightness' has become a less useful cognitive asset to Australians than 'tolerance and plurality'.

Today, Aussie kids are less interested in defending a medieval European truth and are more interested in designing new Aussie truths that are useful and relevant to life in the Third Millennium.

6

AUTHORITY to SOVEREIGNTY

If you don't do your own thinking someone else will do it for you.

WHEN THINKING about thinking, there are two contrasting approaches we can bear in mind: authoritarian and sovereign.

The authoritarian approach is all about someone else doing your thinking for you. That's where THEY say: 'Do what you are told! Trust us. We know what is best for you. We are the chosen ones. We are right and you are wrong. You wouldn't understand. Do not question our authority. When we want your opinion we'll give it to you.' And so on.

The sovereign approach is all about you doing your own thinking for yourself. That's where YOU say: 'Why? Why should I do as you say? Where do you get your authority? Why is this so? Why? Why? Why? What have you not told me What bits have you left out? What proof do you have to offer? I'll think about your proposition and I'll let you know what have decided. I reject your claim to authority over my mind. I abhor your attempt to bully me. I assert my individual sovereignty as a thinker.' And so on.

On sovereign thinkers, religions, belief systems and PTV

It is important to emphasise here that it is the right of a sovereign thinker to think what he likes and to believe what he wishes as long

39

as they do not prevent other sovereign thinkers from doing the same.

A thinker respects the right of individuals to believe in any of the wide variety of human belief systems and religions which are a testimony to the richness, imagination and diversity of human thinking.

Many people derive benefits from believing in UFOs, angels, gods and goddesses, supreme beings, trinities, earthly incarnations or heavenly reincarnations, stars, fortune-tellers, dreams, scientific discoveries, miracles, snake-handling and so on.

One respects these believers in the way Voltaire found he could respect others without having to agree with them. What a thinker does not respect, but fears, is PTV.

For example, one respects the sovereign right of a Christian to believe in Jesus or a Muslim to believe in Allah or an Atheist to believe in nothing. One does not respect an authoritarian Christian or Muslim or Atheist infected with PTV who feels that their belief is 'the truth' and others should be made to 'toe the line or else'! A truth may be right enough for the person who uses it but not right enough to force another person to use it.

In the past few chapters we've been looking at some of the consequences of the authoritarian approach to thinking proceeding from the ideas of Plato, Aristotle and Aquinas. But the richness of human thinking has produced other alternatives and now we can examine the ideas of some who have given their support to the sovereign approach to thinking. There are many, of course, but let's meet one of my personal heroes. This man, like Thomas Aquinas, was also a monk. He was only a peasant German monk yet he defied the greatest authoritarian power in history.

The sovereign thinker

'It is not safe to act against your own conscience'. So said Martin Luther, and with those words began the world's biggest movement away from authoritarianism towards individual sovereignty of thinking.

Luther's rebellion against the authority of the Pope provided the trigger that set off a chain of events which went on long after he died. His challenge to authoritarianism led on to the splitting of the Church, the destruction of the Pope's temporal power, the bursting of the Church's monopoly on The Truth and a greater freedom of people to question things without automatically being treated as heretics. Those of us who cherish personal freedom owe a lot to Luther. What kind of man would defy a pope?

Martin Luther was born in 1483 into a peasant mining family in Germany. At 14 he showed sufficient promise to be prepared for university. By then his father had risen to be manager of group of smelting works and could afford for his son Martin to read law.

So Martin went to Germany's top University of Erfurt and graduated in law, second in his class. Everyone knew that he had a promising law career ahead of him. But no, Martin changed his mind and one day he suddenly decided to join an Augustinian monastery and altered his direction from law to theology.

He began to absorb the predestination ideas of Saint Augustin that men are sinners (Original Sin) and are therefore predestined to whatever God has in store for them. Such a point-of-view reduces the role the Church plays in mediating a person's salvation. At that time, Rome claimed that it, and it alone, had the only ticket to salvation. If you wanted to get to Heaven then you bought your ticket from its representatives on the only flights scheduled to get there. 'You fly with us. You buy our ticket or you don't go to Heaven at all! That's it. Take it or leave it. You're in or you're out'.

Absolute power corrupts absolutely

Brother Martin was already dissatisfied with the Church's claim to being God's exclusive travel agent and so on his visit to Rome he was deeply depressed and revolted upon seeing the spoils of the 'indulgences' scheme, collected from the faithful and displayed in the decadence and opulence of the court of Pope Leo X.

Today, we are used to modern popes who live in a much more tolerant and multi-cultural world. A lot has changed since the 14th century John XXII said that to deny Aquinas was tantamount to heresy. Could you ever imagine the 20th century John XXIII saying such a thing?

The papacy is an extremely difficult job – yet Papal prestige is now at an all-time high. Most modem popes appear to have been men of goodwill who seem to have tried very hard to balance the enormous burden of their office with the exigencies of a free society. That they have done so with such popular success is an extraordinary example of modern leadership.

Examples:

- John XXIII said, 'I am not infallible', and called Vatican II to demonstrate it.

- Paul VI showed great compassion to clergy opposing celibacy, releasing them from their vows.

- John Paul I wanted to clean up the Vatican bank, for which some, like investigative journalist David Yallop, say he was murdered.

- John Paul II was wounded and very nearly assassinated for helping Ronald Reagan to defeat the 'evil' Soviet Empire.

Today's popes are popular superstars who draw huge crowds wherever they go. But this was not always so. In the past, why did so many men, on securing the papacy, become corrupt?

Many have written about the extremes of papal corruption throughout history. Lord Acton wrote on the papacy that, 'Power corrupts and absolute power corrupts absolutely', and it may explain the long history of the papacy's *libido dominandi*, its insatiable lust for power.

Luther's pope was one of the most infamous. He was the youngest cardinal ever. Given a Red Hat for his 13th birthday he became pope when he was 38. It is recorded that as the triple tiara hit his head, Pope

Leo X turned to his illegitimate cousin, Giulio de Medici, and exclaimed, 'Now I can really enjoy myself!'

And he did!

Leo took papal greed to new heights that trivialise the worst corporate excesses of the 1990s. Instead of giving everything up for Christ, Leo grabbed everything he could, in Christ's name. History records the following:

- Leo had 683 courtiers on his payroll, an orchestra, a theatre and a menagerie of wild animals including a white elephant that would bow to Leo three times.

- Leo gave Bacchanalian banquets of 65 courses featuring such delicacies as peacock tongues, nightingales flying out of pies and naked boys jumping out of puddings.

- Flaunting canon law, Leo planned hunting trips for weeks on end.

- His Roman brothels, with 7,000 registered prostitutes in a population of 50,000 still didn't bring in enough income for Pope Leo.

- He was a gambler and big spender, borrowing vast sums from bankers at 40 per cent interest.

- Although simony – the buying and selling of sacred things – was a crime, Leo invented 2,150 papal offices and positions and auctioned them off. Cardinal's Red Hats went for around 30,000 ducats. And so on.

The St Peter's scam

But it was Leo's ultimate act of obscene greed and blasphemy that finally pushed our hero Luther into action. In 1517 Pope Leo X, in cahoots with Prince Albert Hohenzollern, pulled a major scam on the cahoots with Prince Albert Hohenzollern, pulled a major scam on the long-suffering German people.

Leo offered to sell Albert the See of Mainz and the Primacy of Germany for 30,000 ducats. But, since Albert didn't have the money they conspired to raise the cash by selling indulgences (tickets to heaven) to the German people, saying the money was going into a building fund for St Peter's in Rome.

Luther's pamphlets

Luther fought back with a new weapon. Luck was on his side. Gutenberg had recently invented the printing press and Luther not only officially submitted his arguments in Latin to ecclesiastical authorities but also wrote them in his native German tongue and published his pamphlets for general distribution to the German people.

This general distribution was a major new development, the importance of which cannot be overemphasised. In one of his pamphlets he described Leo's papacy as:-

'...more corrupt than any Babylon or Sodom ever was. It is a distressing and terrible thing to see the Head of Christendom, who boasts of being he Vicar of Christ and successor to St Peter, living in a worldly pomp that no King or Emperor can equal; so that in him who calls himself most holy and most spiritual, there is more worldliness than in the world itself.'

Distribution of Luther's pamphlets to the general public broke the Church's monopoly on information and his arguments directly challenged the Pope's authority. The people and the local German princes had had enough! They stood behind Luther and protected him from the wrath of Pope Leo who, of course, excommunicated him. When Luther received his copy of the Pope's Bull of Excommunication, he simply burnt it in defiance.

Inventor of the media

'The die is cast. I despise the fury and favour of Rome. I will have no reconciliation with the Pope for all eternity.' These words are enough to make Martin Luther one of the greatest sovereign thinkers in history.

Using the new technology of the printing press to spread his ideas, Luther became the first thinker ever to bring his argument to the general public. His example, soon followed by others like Calvin, began the unravelling of the authority of Rome that led to the Reformation.

If Gutenberg was the inventor of the printing press, perhaps Martin Luther can be considered the inventor of the media, free speech and the right of individuals to think for themselves.

It may be that the Internet is the next biggest leap for sovereign thinkers since the printing press.

With 250 million users, perhaps the Net is becoming (faster than any other in history) the new medium that will provide a fresh hope for individuals who wish to think for themselves; and who, like Brother Martin, wish to defy the authoritarianism that still exists in many of today's institutions, in Big Government, Big Religion and Big Business.

7

TRUTHS

'If we all worked on the assumption that what is accepted as true is really true, there would be little hope of advance.'

Orville Wright

'I formerly thought that when a tendency to produce the two sexes in equal numbers was advantageous to the species, it would follow from natural selection, but I now see the whole problem is so intricate that it is safer to leave its solution to the future'.

Charles Darwin

THE TRUTH DOES NOT exist in science. There ARE truths in science but there is no such thing as one ABSOLUTE truth. There are only truths that are more likely than other truths.

Science is uncertain. You cannot prove anything in science (in the absolute sense) because science is based on evidence. And, as time passes, there is always more and more evidence.

In science, at any particular time, the balance of evidence supports one point of view or 'truth' as being more likely than any other 'truth'. But, as history has shown, new generations of scientists soon find new evidence, have new ideas and design new paradigms – new ways of looking at the world.

This phenomenon is so well respected by scientists that, as Darwin said in the quote above, they can rely on it happening. Three generations later, Sir Ronald Fisher, the geneticist and father of modern statistics, solved the problem over which Darwin had deliberately procrastinated.

So, science then updates itself by displacing the previous truth with the new, 'more likely' truth. This is the scientific process; the search for more likely truths, that continues and continues on into the future. This uncertainty of science accounts for a lot of its progress.

Replacing old truths with new truths

As mentioned earlier, the prevailing truth before Galileo was Aristotle's view that the earth was the centre of the universe. With the telescope that he invented, Galileo was able to produce evidence that the earth was not the centre but was in orbit around the sun. So, science updates itself and replaces Aristotle' truth with Galileo's new 'sun truth'.

Another more recent example is that of cosmologist George Smoot. He and his COBE satellite team received worldwide recognition for providing evidence of the 'wrinkles in time' that now prove the Big Bang theory to be a fact. So science is now updating itself.

Competing truths are giving way to this new 'more likely truth' because of the weight of evidence provided by the COBE satellite. We now see scientists like David Spergal, the proponent of a competing theory (the textures version of topological defect theory) declaring after the release of the COBE evidence, 'We're dead.'

Even noted physicist Stephen Hawking was willing to admit the COBE discovery was 'the most important of the century, perhaps of all time'. That today's entire universe has grown out of one particle smaller than a proton, as the result of a Big Bang 15 billion years ago, and is expected to go on expanding 'for ever', is no longer a theory. It's a new scientific truth. Watch this space!

Crick and Watson

It has often been said that Einstein's accomplishment in formulating the General Theory of Relativity unaided by a computer is the greatest feat of thinking ever performed by a human brain. It's also said that 'two heads are better than one'. If that is so, then perhaps the greatest feat of thinking ever performed by any two human brains was in 1953 when two scientists, Francis Crick from England and James Watson from America, together cracked the code of codes, for which they jointly received the Nobel Prize.

During the war, after a German bomb blew up his physics laboratory, a young physicist joined the Royal Navy. After the war, Francis Crick switched to biology. He was around 30.

Crick was an atheist. He wanted to expose the 'mysteries' of the illusion of vitalism. He later said:

'My own motives I never had any doubt about; I was very clear in my mind. I chose what we now call molecular biology, though the term wasn't common then, certainly I didn't know it – but I would have said the borderline between the living and the non-living. That was the phrase I had in my mind. '

Horace Freeland Judson's excellent comprehensive history, *The Eighth Day of Creation* (Penguin, London 1979), quotes Crick in his application for his research grant as having written:

'The particular field which excites my interest is the division between the living and the non-living, as typified by, say, proteins, viruses, bacteria, and the structure of chromosomes. The eventual goal, which is somewhat remote, is the description of these activities in terms of their structure; i.e., the spatial distribution of their constituent atoms, in so far as this may prove possible. This might be called the chemical physics of biology.'

He won his grant for research at Cambridge University's famous Cavendish Laboratory.

James Watson was a young Indiana University biology postgraduate. He was also a member of a group of American research scientists who gathered each summer at Cold Spring Harbor on Long Island, an hour out of New York.

In 1944, a short book called *What is Life?* was published by the famous physicist, Erwin Schrodinger. In it, Schrodinger, founder of quantum mechanics, speculated on the physical basis of the gene, its atomic and molecular structure. As a result of reading this book, James Watson once wrote, 'I became polarised towards finding out the secret of the gene'. As his work progressed, Watson became convinced that if he wanted to find the structure of the gene then he had to learn X-ray diffraction techniques so he sailed to England to study there.

Another truth discovered

In October 1951, Crick and Watson met at Cambridge. Crick, 31, was just a research student and Watson, 23, a visitor. They instantly hit it off and became intellectual mountain-climbers, each helping the other up and up.

They could be seen everywhere in animated conversation having tea, in hallways, in laboratories, in the local pub – eventually they were given a room to work in together so as not to disturb the rest of the researchers! Says Crick, 'We must have got the reputation by that time of talking together rather a lot.'

Watson and Crick launched two separate attacks in parallel on the structure of DNA. The first ended in disaster. The second was a success beyond anything they had hoped for. The project required an enormous amount of intellectual effort and research, involving many critical contributions by a number of other researchers. Finally, Crick and Watson cracked the genetic code. They published their ideas in the first of three articles in Nature, on 25 April 1953. It was a three-page article entitled, 'Molecular Structure of Nucleic Acids'. The article included the first published diagram of the molecular structure of their now famous double helix (which looks a bit like a ladder you might find in M.C. Escher's closet).

The code of life

The universal system of all life on this planet is based on a fundamental code and that code was broken by Francis Crick and James Watson in 1953. Since these men unravelled the molecular structure of the gene our world has undergone a continuing and exploding series of revolutionary insights. These scientific developments show no sign of slowing down and nothing can ever be the same.

Prior to 1953 one could still, credibly, hold on to the belief that life itself was ultimately a mysterious thing. One could still, as a thinker, speculate about the origins and 'mysteries' of life. To do so today, it may be argued, is an admission of ignorance, laziness or both.

Digital genes

We now know that genes are digital. They are long strings of pure digital information. Like CDs and computers, the code of life – all life – is mighty digital in its internal structure. Whereas the binary code of computers has two symbols, in life the code is quaternary with four symbols. Otherwise they're digitally the same.

What, then, is the essential difference between the machine code of a computer and that of your genes? The answer is: none!

The famous Oxford Darwinist, Richard Dawkins, author of *The Selfish Gene*, has explained that our genetic code is so digital to the core that you could encode, with word-for-word accuracy the whole of the bible in those parts of the human genome that are at present filled with junk DNA.

In his recent book, *River Out of Eden*, he illustrates the strongly digital nature of genes with characteristic clarity and wit:-

'The following science-fiction plot is feasible, given a technology that differs from today's only in being a little speeded up. Professor Jim Crickson has been kidnapped by an evil foreign power and forced to work in its biological warfare labs. To save civilisation it is vitally important that he should communicate some top-secret information to the outside world, but all normal channels of communication are denied him. Except one.

'The DNA code consists of sixty-four triplet 'codons', enough for a complete upper- and lower-case English alphabet plus ten numerals, a space character and a full stop or period. Professor Crickson takes a virulent influenza virus off the laboratory shelf and engineers into its genome the complete text of his message to the outside world, in perfectly formed English sentences. He repeats his message over and over again in the engineered genome, adding an easily recognisable 'flag' sequence – say, the first ten prime numbers. He then infects himself with the virus and sneezes in a room full of people.

'A wave of flu sweeps the world, and medical labs in distant lands set to work to sequence its genome in an attempt to design a vaccine. It soon becomes apparent that there is a strange repeated pattern in the genome. Alerted by the prime numbers – which cannot have arisen spontaneously – somebody tumbles to the idea of employing code-breaking techniques. From there it would be short work to read the full English text of Professor Crickson's message, sneezed around the world.'

So, if life is digital and knowable, the 'mystery of mysteries' ha evaporated. What effect does that have on us as sovereign thinkers? In what way has the feat of Watson and Crick helped to free us from authoritarianism? In what way has the work of these two scientists added a quantum leap to our freedom as sovereign thinkers?

Knowledge and power

One of this book's themes is the connection between knowledge and power. Knowledge is power and thinking is the source of knowledge. Thinking is also the source of power.

Like Luther's use of the media, the genetic revelation of Crick and Watson is another huge victory for knowledge over authority. A thinker no longer needs a 'priest of the knowledge' with special mystical powers to explain 'the meaning of life'. It is now readily explicable and easily understandable by the individual without any need for an intermediary who retains special 'supernatural powers' for himself. To the sovereign thinker, this is a huge dividend of personal freedom.

No powerbase likes to surrender its power. It would be naive to think so. However the old supernatural powerbases, still operating in today's world, have lost most of their temporal power and what little remains is rapidly disintegrating at an astonishing rate of acceleration.

In some ways it is ironic how the uncertain truths of science have so overtaken the certainty of The Truth. Even the highest claims of occult certainty seem thin and puerile compared to the demonstrable achievements of science.

A supernatural assumption or a scientific demonstration

Perhaps the ultimate claim of occult certainty was made in 1950. Around the same time that Crick and Watson were heading for Cambridge, a mystical methodology was producing a fresh discovery in Rome.

There has only been one infallible claim ever made by a pope since Pius IX proclaimed the doctrine of papal infallibility in 1870. An Italian priest, Eugenio Pacelli as Pius XII, suddenly, in 1950, asserted his doctrine of The Assumption.

Speaking *ex cathedra* and claiming infallibility he decided that Mary was physically assumed into heaven. He professed that not only was Mary's physical body actually taken into heaven, but also that this claim was the supreme statement of certainty, that only a Supreme Pontiff could make.

He even added that his recondite discovery was so certain a 'fact' that if any Catholics ever wished to automatically excommunicate themselves from the church, they only had to wilfully doubt his declaration and they were out. Finito.

In his *anathema*, he said:-

'1f anyone, which God forbid, should dare wilfully to deny or call in doubt that which We have defined, let him know that he has fallen away completely from the divine and Catholic faith...'

Leaving aside the impertinence of this assertion and the total lack of any evidence to support it, Pius XII's 'aeronautical invention' is relatively tame compared with those of scientists in the field.

By contrast, for example, a fallible, uncertain Swiss scientist, Daniel Bernoulli, discovered the principle of the aerofoil that today enables a pope to fly around the world in a 747, faster than a bullet, along with the entire College of Cardinals!

Throw in a movie, a reasonable meal and some French Champagne and it beats riding around on a cloud any day. Also, there are no threats of excommunication involved in international air travel, just the occasional loss of baggage.

The end of the Mystical Millennium

More and more brainusers are turning to science for answers to questions that were once the exclusive domain of the supernatural powerbases. In Australia, the latest government census has confirmed this accelerating rejection of religions, sects and cults.

As we leave the Mystical Millennium, the superficial, childish mythologies of the truth-merchants and medieval magicians are being left behind. The information-rich revelations of science are empowering more thinkers than ever before to choose sovereignty over authority.

1953 is important because it was the definitive end of the Mystical Millennium. It was the last of the big 'mysteries' to be explained. Though there may always be many interesting questions to be asked and answered, after Crick and Watson no thinker need ever delegate her or his authority to a supernatural magician, ever again. If she or he CHOOSES to do so for some other reason, that is their right and privilege.

The greatest thinkers

Francis Crick and James Watson are two of history's greatest intellectual superstars. Never have two thinkers explained so much. Their discovery of the digital gene has cleared away many veils of mystery.

Many other scientists have since built on Crick and Watson's original ideas and more work will be done in the future. The human genome mapping project is nearing its climax. But, as a contribution to the freedom of individual thinkers, Crick and Watson's achievement dwarfs those of the 'truth hackers', Aristotle and Aquinas, and provides a major blow to PTV.

As you ponder these things, what is the most liberating idea, discovery or truth that you can think of which has made it possible for you to be more of a sovereign thinker?

8

ANTIDOTE

SO FAR WE have looked at PTV, how it arose and how it spread via the medieval Church into the Western education system. We saw how this truth-driven education system with its emphasis on 'the search for certainty' was exported around the world, and how your own brain may have become infected.

The effects of PTV

How does PTV work to inhibit your abilities as sovereign thinker? Well, as a cognitive disease, PIV in your brain can produce a number of deleterious effects. Let's look at just four manifestations of PTV:

- Brain Vain (opinion, pride and conceit)
- Righteous and Sightless (consequence blindness)
- Space Glutton (output-mania)
- Lazy Critic (mistake-phobia).

Brain vain

A brain vain thinker is one who is suffering from opinion pride. This PTV-infected brainuser is unable to see a better way of looking at things. Because the brain vain thinker is so proud of her or his own opinion they find it difficult to do any other kind of thinking but to defend it.

The more intelligent the brain vain thinker, the more they may suffer from this kind of cognitive conceit. Very bright thinkers who are PTV-infected may be only using their brainpower to defend their opinion. They are unable to escape from their viewpoint to look for a better one.

Righteous and Sightless

The righteous brain is blind to consequences. PTV may have so incapacitated a True Believer that he is unable to see the results of his actions. In the belief of being 'morally right' any action is justified by the righteous and sightless, regardless of what follows. This is a very dangerous condition and so often fatal.

Millions have rushed headlong into death because of Queen and country. Millions have been killed because they are 'infidels', 'Jews', 'Catholics' or 'Protestants'. 'I-am-right-and-you-are-wrong' is the hallmark of the righteous and sightless condition.

In 1994, John Paul II urged all Roman Catholic cardinals to reflect on this aspect of the Church's history. He wrote to them asking them to seize the unique beginning of the new millennium to recognise the 'dark side of its history'. He asked:

'How can one remain silent about the many forms of violence perpetrated in the name of the faith – wars of religion, tribunals of the Inquisition and other forms of violations of the rights of persons?'

Space Glutton

In a meeting, the space glutton always takes up considerably more than his or her fair share of air-time. Space gluttons may suffer from output mania, the inability to shut up.

Gathering input by listening to the opinions of others is an important cognitive skill which is crippled in the space glutton. PTV may allow the thinker to wreak such enthusiasm for her own ideas that she is quite unable to listen to those of others.

In business, much creativity and productivity is lost in meetings due to those suffering from this condition. This condition is disastrous for those in sales or management.

Lazy Critic

Lazy critics suffer from mistake-phobia, the morbid fear of ever making a mistake. The PTV-infected brain has an aversion to ever being wrong. It comes from our medieval habit of looking at the world through the concept of 'right' and 'wrong' (not shared as much by other cultures like the Japanese).

When a sovereign thinker tries to create something, he never really knows what will happen. There is always risk and uncertainty. This risk is enough to keep the mistake-phobiac hiding in inertia. As an effective disguise the mistake-phobiac often assumes the role of 'the critic'.

Taking pot-shots from the relative safety of his bunker of reluctance, the lazy critic simply waits for another thinker to make a mistake and then the whingeing begins.

These are a few of the cognitive conditions caused by PTV. There are many others. The purpose of the School of Thinking is to help brainusers deal with these conditions.

The brain software

You can do this by using the brain software which we developed in the School of Thinking. This is the first real software for the brain ever invented to overcome PTV. The brain software is provided in Part Two of this book and is for you to use at school, at work, at home and at play.

It consists of four software packages for your brain. These

software packages contain 15 mind-tools. These mind-tools can be used by the brainuser in an ever-widening repertoire of combinations to produce a virtually unlimited number of effects.

The neuro-software is expressed in a four-part code: SDNT CVSTOBVS QRH PRR. Each abbreviation stands for a specific piece of brain software which will be dealt with in the following chapters.

Once it is programmed into your brain, the neuroware helps to neutralise PTV by giving you, the brainuser, a simple way to increase your awareness of the thinking strategies that are available to you in any situation that comes your way.

Brain training

Over the next 24 hours, try to notice at least one example of each of the following:

Brain Vain (opinion pride and conceit)

✎ ....

Righteous and Sightless (consequence blindness)

✎ ....

Space Glutton (output-mania)

✎ ....

Lazy Critic (mistake-phobia)

✎ ....

SUMMARY of
PART ONE

The main ideas in Part One are:-

☐ The Truth, the idea that there is an objective truth, was invented by Plato. Strong defence of The Truth diminishes the thinker's ability to escape from his viewpoint to find a much better one. This condition is called PTV, Plato Truth Virus.

☐ Aristotle imbedded PTV in his syllogism. This was picked up by Thomist doctrine and became the basis of logic. Western education has made a god out of logic and the 'search for certainty'.

☐ The Western education system was set up by the medieval Church and spread throughout Europe and exported to other parts of the world. Even today, children are sent to school, their young brains programmed with the logic operating system, and then they're given the impression that all they have to do in life is "get the right answer" or "tell the truth".

☐ Only Microsoft's global export of Bill Gates' DOS/Windows has ever rivalled the Vatican's global export of Thomas Aquinas' PTV.

☐ PTV is ubiquitous. Manifestations of PTV can be annoying, as in Space Gluttons and Bores, or fatal, as in Bullies and Righteous and Sightless thinkers. Over 26 million humans have been destroyed in the last hundred years directly as a result of PTV.

Unfair conclusion

It is only with the unfair advantage of hindsight that one is able to look back on the evolution of our thinking habits and consider the consequences that they may have produced.

> **?** Did Plato ever realise what might happen as a consequence of the ideas that emerged from those Bacchanalian dinner parties he attended on those hot Athenian summer nights?

> **?** Did Saint Thomas Aquinas ever anticipate how rigorously later popes would prosecute his ideas and make them the core doctrine of the greatest education enterprise in history?

To be fair, I don't see how they could. Plato and Thomas were not villains. I imagine they were just doing what interested them most at the time and hoping for a modest amount of success.

Could Bill Gates ever have known he would become the richest businessman in the world when he first developed DOS/Windows? In his book he says he once remarked to Paul Allen that a million dollars was a huge amount of money, and he could never imagine having more than that.

Microsoft (at the time of writing) has been valued at $320 billion...

Part II

BRAIN
SOFTWARE

9

SOFTWARE SOLUTIONS

IMAGINE THAT YOU owned the best music system that money could buy. Suppose you paid £10,000 for an amplifier/equaliser and another £5,000 for a CD/cassette player, plus £20,000 for the best speakers you could get hold of. You could now boast that you owned the best music hardware system in your street, maybe even the best in your town.

Now, imagine you only had one solitary Patsy Kline CD to play on your ultra-hi fi hardware. There's nothing wrong with Pats but a diet of I Fall To Pieces and Your Cheatin' Heart may be somewhat limiting when it comes to long-term musical entertainment.

These same limitations face us when we boast possession of a necktop computer yet only have one piece of thinking software, logic. Logic is useful enough for labelling and mail-sorting and dealing with the past but it's not nearly enough to help us cope with the challenges of the future.

We do need some different software for our brain to help us survive in rapidly-changing environments and increasingly competitive and shrinking global markets. We also need more brain software because we're not *happy* being stuck with what we have at present.

Brainpower and intelligence

Brainpower is how you use tools, like software, to enhance your intelligence. These tools are higher-order cognitive tools that help us think about what we should think about. Sometimes this 'thinking about thinking' is called by cognitive scientists, meta-cognition.

There are two main types of intelligences:

* Data Intelligence; and
* Game Intelligence.

Data Intelligence

Data intelligence is the role that information plays in thinking.

Data intelligence is only necessary for the relatively dumb, unthinking reaction to situations: 'What do I do next?'

Game Intelligence

Game intelligence is the role of strategies, clever moves, clever ideas, ploys and tricks that are the product of thinking about and exploring the information.

Game intelligence goes a step further, where the individual asks himself, 'What do I think about next?' *before* asking,'What do I do next?'

Brain software is a mind-tool which permits the brainuser to go a step even further by allowing him or her to ask, 'How do I think better about what I should think about next?'

Tools are important for intelligence. Tools, like a laptop, are not just the result of intelligence but they actually ENDOW intelligence on the user. When you give someone a laptop you increase or enhance their chances of arriving at more intelligent moves.

'Anthropologists have long recognised that the advent of tool use accompanied a major increase in intelligence'

...observes Daniel Dennett, Director of the Center for Cognitive Studies at Tufts University and author of Consciousness Explained.

Commenting on the value of mind-tools in developing the user's intelligence, he says:-

'Tool use is a two-way sign of intelligence. Not only does it require intelligence to recognise and maintain a tool but tool use CONFERS intelligence on those who are lucky enough to be given the tool. The better designed the tool, the more potential intelligence it confers on the user.'

Cognitive science

Since the 1970s brought the explosion of the Information Revolution and the rise of personal computers we've become even more interested in the brain and how it works. 'What is intelligence?' and 'How can we improve it?' are questions being asked in a whole new field of science devoted to these things called – cognitive science.

Cognitive science is concerned with the processes of sensing (seeing, hearing, smelling, touching); storing information (memory) and recall; reasoning, planning and intelligent action. It also includes areas like AI (Artificial Intelligence) and robotics In other words, thinking – both in animals and machines.

Like all human traits – height, strength, sexuality and looks, etc., intelligence is distributed unequally. Some people have more intelligence than you do and some have less than you do – and, of course, the same applies to me.

How's your brainpower?

Here is a simple audit for you to rate your own brainpower. It was designed by Dr Eric Bienstock, who ran the School of Thinking (SOT) in New York. Eric based this checklist on the SOT's Learn-To-Think coursebook. How do you rate your own brainpower?

BRAINPOWER TEST

INSTRUCTIONS: Answer each of the following questions, scoring either 3, 2, 1, or O points for each answer depending on your objective estimate of how often you actually do what is stated. Use your best guess of the following criteria for scoring:-

3 points = 90% of the time (nearly always)
2 points = 70% of the time (mostly)
1 point = 40% of the time (often)
O points = 10% of the time (hardly ever)

SCORE

.... My judgements of ideas are based on the value of the idea rather than on my emotions at the time.

.... I judge ideas not just as 'good' or 'bad' but also as 'interesting' if they can lead on to better ideas.

.... I consider all factors in a situation before choosing, deciding or planning.

.... I consider all factors first, before picking out the ones that matter most.

.... When I create a rule I see to it that it is clearly understood and possible to obey.

.... I try to see the purpose of rules I have to obey, even if I don't like the rules.

.... I look at consequences of my decisions or actions not only as they affect me but also as they affect other people.

.... I look at a wide range of possible consequences before deciding which consequences to bother about.

.... On the way to a final objective I establish a chain of smaller objectives each one following on from the previous one.

.... The objectives I set are near enough, real enough and possible enough for me to really try to reach them.

.... In planning, I know exactly what I want to achieve.

.... I keep my plans as simple and direct as possible.

.... I know exactly why I have chosen something as a priority.

.... I try to get as many different ideas as possible first, before starting to pick out the priorities.

.... I will go on looking for alternatives until I find one I really like.

.... While most people look for alternatives when they are not satisfied, I look for them deliberately even when I am satisfied.

.... I am able to tell myself the real reason behind a decision I make.

.... Before making a decision, I consider the factors, look at the consequences, get clear about the objectives, assess the priorities, and search for possible alternatives.

.... I am able to see the other person's point-of-view whether I agree with it or not.

.... I am able to spell out the differences and similarities between different viewpoints.

TOTAL SCORE.................

INTERPRETATION

This is not a scientific test. It's just an audit or checklist to help you take stock of your thinking, that's all! A trained thinker can direct his or her thinking and use it in a deliberate manner to produce an effect. To a trained and skilled thinker, thinking is a tool that can be used at will and the use of this tool is practical. This ability to use 'thinking as a skill' is the sort of thinking ability that is required to get things DONE.

* If your total score in this test was between 51 and 60 points, you already possess superior brainpower.

* If you scored between 31 and 50 points, you have better than average brainpower.

* If you scored between O and 30, you possess no additional brainpower other than the natural thinking ability that most people have.

10

BRAINPOWER & COGNETICS

THE DESIGN MODEL for the mind-tools presented in this book is what I have called cognetics. You don't have to worry about the name but if you don't come up with a fancy name in science, nobody takes you seriously.

Cognetics comes from cognitive cybernetics. Cognitive means to do with how the brain 'minds' and cybernetics has to do with 'feedback'. Cognetics brain software – 'neuroware' – consists of higher order executive patterns that you can use deliberately to:-

1. Take control of your attention; and
2. Manipulate your own perception.

Once it is programmed into your brain, the brain software gives you, the brainuser, a simple way to increase your awareness of the thinking strategies that are available to you in a situation.

For example, suppose you are dealing with a problem and you are currently aware of only three strategies you can use - Strategy A, Strategy B or Strategy C. For you then, your intelligent behaviour is limited to a choice from those three strategies.

But what if you could deliberately make yourself aware of six or nine or twelve strategies you could use in that situation? Obviously you would be able to choose an even higher level of intelligent behaviour due to your increased options.

Problems and opportunities

Brainpower or cognetics is this deliberate use and application of thinking software. In cognetics, you can choose from a range of cognitive strategies to solve any problem that confronts you or to explore any opportunity you desire.

A problem is a situation which may require a solution, a way out, an option, a cure or a new approach. An opportunity is a situation that may need to be explored, a plan that needs to be worked out, an idea that needs to be developed, a possibility that needs testing.

Your problems or opportunities are often personal, business, family, recreational, academic, scientific, physical, or philosophical. (Thinking like old Aristotle, there!)

When we ask businesspeople about their problem/ opportunity areas they nearly always say: career or purpose in life, time and stress, getting a better balance between professional and personal life, money issues, bringing more creativity and flexibility into their company.

Here are some of the situations SOT members have worked on during their Clever Brainuser training:

OPPORTUNITIES: to buy some land; to get a better job; to improve their knowledge of South East Asia; to learn acting; to play the piano again; to grow their business; to go back to school, to raise their income, to give up smoking, to improve their golf.

PROBLEMS: to pay the mortgage; to cope with a difficult boss; to save my marriage; to choose between academic courses; to overcome my fear of using the telephone in selling; to speak in public; to make new friends; to lose weight.

Intelligent behaviour equals strategies and options

If you wish to order take-away food but you only have a pizza menu then your choice is limited to pizza. But if you have menus from 10 different restaurants including sushi, health food, Spanish, seafood, Thai, TexMex, French and pizza, etc. then you can eat much better. The key is to keep yourself aware of a broader menu of options.

The brain software – SDNT CVSTOBVS QRH PRR – (introduced in the next chapter) will keep you aware of strategic options you can use in situations that confront you. This book will explain these strategies and your increased skills will give you a simple way to raise your Game Intelligence by at least 100 per cent and minimise the effects of PTV.

The four-part brain software package provides your brain with 15 mind-tools. These mind-tools can be used by the brainuser in an ever-widening repertoire of combinations to produce a virtually unlimited number of effects. Just as the carpenter can use a dozen or so tools to perform a wide range of effects, so can the brainuser.

11

NECKTOP

APPARENTLY I was the first to coin the term 'necktop computer'. In the eighties, while on the lecture circuit in the US and Europe, I was invited to give the keynote address to a series of IBM conferences in Monte Carlo.

There, I introduced CVSTOBVS as 'software for the brain' and referred to the brain as a necktop computer. It highly amused the executives in the audience so I kept it in my talks for a laugh. Now it's passe.

Soon there will be 400 million PC users worldwide. Today's PCs are up to 20 gigabytes where a byte is just a single storage unit of information (at eight bits) or about one printed character. 20 gigs is 20 million kilobytes or 20 billion bytes. So, 400 million PCs multiplied by 20 billion bytes is ... Wow! That's a lot of personal computer power.

How many necktop users are there? There are presently (Dec 1999) about 6 billion necktop users on planet earth. This number is increasing at the rate of three necktop users ever second or 1.7 million every week.

In your brain a byte is, say, the strength of a synapse but your necktop has rather more than 20 billion bytes or synapses. It is a vast network of about 100 billion neurons (quite possibly even ten times as many, we're not sure yet) and each one of your neurons has up to 50,000 connecting wires (dendrites) with synapses.

One hundred billion neurons multiplied by 50,000 synapses multiplied by 5.7 billion necktops equals... whew! That's a lot of brainpower on the planet.

Professor Jacob Schwartz of the Courant Institute of Mathematical Sciences at New York University has put some figures together to give some idea of the capacity of your brain. He says that, 'Rough quantitative guesses lead us to estimate that the long-term memory available to the brain is about 10,000 trillion bytes' and that 'the computing rate needed to emulate the entire brain on a neuron-by-neuron basis may be as high as 1,000,000 trillion arithmetical operations per second'.

Dr Schwartz goes on to say that, 'It is interesting to compare these exceedingly coarse estimates with corresponding figures for the largest supercomputer systems likely to be developed over the next decade. These will probably not attain speeds in excess of one trillion arithmetical operations per second which is about one-millionth of the computation rate that we have estimated for your brain'.

You and I, with our human brains, are so preposterously overendowed with thinking hardware that it's almost impossible to comprehend. But let's try.

What if you were the major shareholder of the world's most intelligent enterprise, a network of ten billion computers linked together as parallel processors, producing a vast intellectual output of global messaging?

Well, you are!

Units of intellect

Take a closer look. The atoms of your brain are called nerve cells or neurons. Each neuron is your fundamental intellectual unit – an information-processing system. The basic product of these units is: messaging.

Neurons are perfectly designed messaging systems. They have two ends: a receiving end and a transmitting end (or an input end and an output end).

At the receiving end, each of your neurons is a convenient, tree-like system of dendrites – input wires – which can receive information from other neurons. A neuron may receive messages from thousands of other neurons and may in turn send its messages out to thousands of other neurons.

Messages in and messages out

Suppose we call a message in, a MI. And, a message out, a MO. So we have MIs and MOs.

A neuron receives MIs (messages in) from other neurons, then sends a MO, a brief electrical pulse lasting about a thousandth of a second along its output wire, the axon. Axon are like telegraph wires that transmit electrical signals along their own length. At the end of its wire the axon's electrical signal is transformed into a chemical output – a neurotransmitter.

A neurotransmitter is a package of chemical information which has an effect on the neuron that receives it in much the same way that a fax or an e-mail is a package of information which has an effect on you when you receive it. The way the chemical package affects the neuron receiving it is by causing change in its electro-chemical activity.

To send or not to send, that's the decision

Just as you may or may not respond to an e-mail or fax you receive, your neuron behaves the same way. Sometimes a neuron responds to a MI. Sometimes it doesn't. When a particular cell sends out its own MO signal it's because it has received enough MIs from other cells to exceed a threshold figure.

Thus each of your nerve cells acts as a tiny decision unit. If the incoming messaging is above a certain level, it responds with a MO. If not, it stays silent. If your neuron does respond to its incoming messages we say it is excited, if it stays silent we say it is inhibited.

You have more than a trillion neurons – tiny molecular computers. Like other computers they have a broad selection of MOs that they can send out. Each of your neurons acts as a unit of control receiving

MIs and sending MOs within the distributed network you call your brain. Each of these units is processing its inputs/outputs at the same time as are all the other units, so they achieve 'parallel computation'.

Your brain is the ultimate parallel processor! Its billions of parallel processing units are constantly taking in information MIs. These messages are processed and changed. Then new information MOs are sent out all over the global network. Your brain is the supreme intelligent enterprise. And guess what, you are the major shareholder.

SDN Search Engine™

START DO NOTICE THINK
START DO NOTICE THINK
START DO NOTICE THINK
START DO NOTICE THINK
START DO NOTICE THINK
START DO NOTICE THINK
START DO NOTICE THINK
START DO NOTICE THINK
START DO NOTICE THINK
START DO NOTICE THINK
START DO NOTICE THINK
START DO NOTICE THINK
START DO NOTICE THINK
START DO NOTICE THINK
START DO NOTICE THINK
START DO NOTICE THINK
START DO NOTICE THINK
START DO NOTICE THINK

12

START

'Taking a new step, uttering a new word, is what people fear most.'

Fyodor Dostoevsky

IT CAN BE VERY difficult to start things. Once you get started there is momentum and feedback but getting started can be difficult. Most races are lost not at the finishing line but at the starting blocks. Why? Because most people never even enter the race! They just never get started. Wasn't it Lao-Tzu who pointed out that all journeys begin with one step?

The start of the sale = customer attention

What is the start of the sale? The start of the sale is Customer Attention. Before a customer can say YES or NO their attention must be on your offer. Fred Herman, author of *KISS: Keep It Simple, Salesman* used to say, 'First, you've got to get the customer's attention'.

Yet, most of the time the vast majority of customers' attention is not focused on your offer at all. Whenever, at any particular moment, the customer's attention is not on your offer then there can be no hope of a sale.

The Check! move

To manage customer attention I designed a new unit of measurement. In my book *NewSell*, which became a best-seller in Australia, I designed a new unit of measurement which I called the Check! move. A Check! move (taken from the game of chess) is simply a customer contact of any kind and is represented by the symbol: C!

For years it's been a common belief in selling that most sales were lost at the close. In other words, salespeople were missing sales because they were not 'closing' them. Our research showed that this is a grand illusion. The whole issue of 'closing the sale' is a nonsense and I have offered a reward of £50,000 to the first person who can prove the salesperson closes the sale.

- FACT: The decision to buy is an electro-chemical event in the brain of the customer and the salesperson does NOT control that event.

- FACT: 99 per cent of sales are not missed at the close at all but at the start.

- FACT: It's the failure to start the sale – to contact a customer by phone, by snail mail, by e-mail, by fax or in person – that is the source of most lost business.

- FACT: 99 per cent of C! moves have never yet been made.

Noting their C! moves (customer contacts) helps salespeople keep a measure of how much energy they are putting out into the marketplace. Focusing on their C! moves helps them to:

1. Raise their energy level and avoid wasting time.

2. Stop their obsession with 'the close' and all the archaic manipulation tactics that customers hate and which have given the selling profession such a bad image.

Focusing on the start – C! – rather than the 'close', reduces the rejection and disappointment salespeople feel which so affect their energy levels. C! allows them to initiate many more customer contacts.

This, of course, always leads to better sales results because the only move that can turn a prospective customer into a client is CHECK! which is enough to make it the most important move in business. As Woody Allen said, *'80 per cent of success is showing up.'*

MBO or MBS?

How to start? Most plans are full of details on how to get to the finishing line but contain little or nothing about how to get to the starting blocks. Yet nothing happens until someone STARTS something. For many years in business we have had MBO or Management By Objectives. Perhaps we also need MBS or Management By Starting.

Many management gurus write books about goal-getting. Maybe they should also write books about 'start-getting' since most of the time, most people never get started.

To start is the fundamental creative act. To change a switch from the OFF position to the ON position is to start something and means something has now been created. It has been said that the most important skill in writing a book is sitting down at the keyboard – getting started.

Strategic act

Strategy is about control. If you are in control you are in a strategic position, if you are out of control you aren't. Starting is a strategic act because we can control starting but we cannot control finishing.

Once we start, many other factors come into play: other people's reactions, the weather, consequences and the unexpected. These may prevent us from finishing. But if we are good at starting then we can always start again, and again, and again. It may be that finishing is simply the repetitive act of starting, and starting again, and starting again, until we declare that we have 'finished'.

Some people are good at starting. Others are good at the follow-up. Some are good at both. What are you better at? Do you see starting as a skill? How can you improve your starting ability? Is it worth it? What would be a better skill to develop than starting? How do you start to start? To start or not to start? To flip the switch or not to flip the switch? To start is to be! I start therefore I am. He who hesitates to start is lost. Start before you leap, etc.

Where to start?

Anywhere is a good place to start. Sir Yehudi Menuhin started playing the violin at home when he was four. Home is a good place to start. He made his professional debut when he was seven, in San Francisco. San Francisco is a good place to start.

In 1962 he started a boarding school for musically talented children, at Stoke d'Abernon, near London. Boarding school is a good place to start. Sir Yehudi's son Jeremy made his debut as a pianist, in Gstaad, in 1965. Dare I say it – Gstaad is a good place to start!

Is there a best place to start? Why?

Is there a worst place to start? Why?

Why start things?

When you start, you begin to overcome inertia. Inertia is the enemy of starting, with its lack of feedback. Once you escape from the spell of inertia you begin to get feedback. Feedback is the food of decision-making and the food of design. You can assess feedback and react to your assessment. Do I like it? Do I not like it? Do I want more? Do I want less?

We are much better at reacting than at proacting. By creating feedback it gives us something to react to and so we can make a decision and proceed. A simple way to create feedback is to start something... anything.

When to start?

There is really only one time to start and that time is the moment called... Now! We need to create as many Now! moments for starting as possible. Just suppose a Now! moment is one second. In other words, let's define the time it takes to start something as one second. Here are some examples:

? How long does it take to pick up the telephone?

ONE SECOND

? How long does it take to press 'send' on an e-mail?

ONE SECOND

? How long does it take to start to get up and go for a walk?

ONE SECOND

? How long does it take to start a Yahoo search on the net?

ONE SECOND

? How long does it take to say 'No'?

ONE SECOND

? How long does it take to start your laptop?

ONE SECOND

? How long does it take to start to contact a customer?

ONE SECOND

There are an unlimited number of things you can start to do in the quite comfortable space of one second. How many Now! moments are there in a day? I'll save you the trouble of the maths: it's 84,000.

Unfortunately we waste most of our Now! moments because we squander most of our time immobilised by inertia because of our Western fear of making 'mistakes'.

Mistake-phobia

Mistake-phobia is the morbid fear of making a mistake. It's an aversion to ever being wrong. It comes from our medieval habit of looking at the world through the concept of 'right' and 'wrong' (not shared by other cultures like the Japanese).

Compared to the Japanese our mistake-phobia causes us to lose countless opportunities on a daily basis in Western countries like Australia, Britain, France and America and it may be one of the biggest single blocks to our increased productivity and potential economic success.

Have a go!

One way to cure mistake-phobia is to accelerate our willingness to have a go, to get started and get busy. When you have a go, one of two things happens:

1. You make a mistake; or
2. You make an un-mistake.

To the brainuser, both these types of feedback are useful.

If you are not afraid of mistakes, if you are not a mistake-phobiac, then you simply assess the feedback and start again. If it was a mistake you try something different. If it was an un-mistake then you can keep going. These are like loops that can be called:

1. IF (mistake) THEN (start again) ELSE (proceed), or
2. IF (un-mistake) THEN (proceed).

Both these outcomes are useful results of starting, they just have different values. Inertia may have no value at all.

This is how we have taught computers to be intelligent. They keep doing something. Anything. They keep busy going through the loops and learning. This is how we learned as children until we were taught to dread making a mistake. If computers were as afraid of making mistakes as we are then they would take as long as us to learn. But they don't. Computers are not afraid of mistakes and are rapidly catching up. Today's cars have more computing power than the whole world had 40 years ago. They are becoming less 'computer-assisted cars and more like 'driveable computers.' Where will computers be in the next 40 years? In the next 400 years?

Lazy critic

Lazy critics suffer from mistake-phobia. The PTV-infected brain will turn the most amazing cognitive somersaults to avoid being 'wrong'. When a brainuser tries to create something, he never really knows what will happen. There is always risk and uncertainty. Risk is enough to keep the mistake-phobiac hiding beneath their inertia.

But, remember, nothing happens until someone STARTS something. Soren Kierkegaard said, 'To dare is to lose one's footing momentarily. To not dare is to lose oneself.' Do you prefer the starter or the critic? How do you feel about mistakes Are you comfortable with them? Or do you fear mistakes? Can you take a risk?

Starting by asking

To ask is one way to start. Mrs Robert Lee Kidd started something simply by walking into the office of the San Francisco Examiner on 2 May 1962 and placing her advertisement which asked for the following:

'I don 't want my husband to die in the gas chamber for a crime he did not commit. I will therefore offer my services for 10 years as a cook, maid or housekeeper to any leading attorney who will defend him and bring about his vindication.'

Her husband had been tried and convicted of the murder of 71-year-old antiques dealer, Albert Clarke. Mr Kidd's bloody fingerprints had been found on the murder weapon, an ornate sword. But Mrs Kidd had insisted her husband was home with her on the night of the crime. One of San Francisco's most eminent attorneys, Vincent Hallinan, responded and proved in court that the sword was not the murder weapon after all. Subsequently, both husband and wife went free. Hallinan graciously refused to take up Mrs Kidd's offer of 10 years service. Ask and receive! Asking is one way of starting.

Ask and receive

Every day, thousands of people start something by putting their ad in the paper asking for something, e.g. a job, a house, a vote, a sale, a friend, etc. By asking, there are literally an unlimited number of ways of getting started.

When did you last put an ad in the paper? What happened? What other ways can you ask? What did you ask for yesterday? What will you ask for today? What will you ask for tomorrow?

Getting started

The hardest part about getting started is... getting started! This is a circular trap that is difficult to get out of and is the cause of a lot of inertia. The way I get started is to write down a list of 10 things I can do to get started, then I just choose the ones I like.

Brain Training

How to get started:

✎ Write down TEN things you wish you could get started on.

✎ Write down TEN things you can do to get started on number 1 on your list.

✎ What can you ask for to start something?

✎ Write an ad you can place to support this request.

✎ If you wish, you can place the ad and discuss the results.

13

DO

NO IDEA IS OF any real value until it gets used. If an idea never gets used, why even know about it?

There's a huge gap between knowing and doing. I have called this gap The Impossible Barrier – and written at length about it in *NewSell*. The reason for identifying this gap is because, so often, knowing something prevents one doing it.

We have something repeated to us and we say, 'Yes, I already know that!' and we turn our attention away. Yet it is the repetition of things we already know that gets us closer to doing it. It has been said that too often the knowers are not the doers and the doers are not the knowers.

Once we move from thought into action we immediately create feedback. Our actions have consequences and it is these consequences that enable us to evaluate the effectiveness of our behaviour. Thinking is not an escape from action, it is simply the basis for it (see Shakespeare's Hamlet...). When in doubt, do something. Anything.

The quest – seek and ye shall find

You may already have noticed that the recurring theme running though all this cognetics training about human information-handling is ESCAPE and MOVEMENT. To the thinker, a creative approach to life means a questioning approach.

Questing was the kind of adventurous modus operandi of the knight of chivalry. Whether on the 'impossible dream', the crusade, or the search for the Holy Grail, the true knight went out seeking challenges and embracing problems. He was a knight, a man of action, a doer, doing what knights do.

Today's knights are no different. Whether a man or woman, the knight of today has the same spirit of questing, only the weapons are different. In Cyberia, the keyboard is mightier than the sword.

Today's cyberknights, like their ancient brothers, are the great questers of the information age. They use search engines rather than siege engines. They don't use chain-mail but they do use e-mail. They surf Cyberia on their laptop instead of sailing to Outremer on their warships. But, they're out there, and this is just the beginning.

Questions are the answer

The skilled thinker, the thinker of action, is a skilled questioner.

Who? What? When? Where? How? Why? Why? Why? The only silly question is the question you don't ask. But what is a question? According to Rochelle Myers, who runs the now-famous Stamford University Graduate School of Management course, Creativity in Business, questions are the following:-

? A question is an opening to creation

? A question is an unsettled and unsettling issue

? A question is an invitation to creativity

? A question is a beginning of an adventure

? A question is a seductive foreplay

? A question is a point of departure

? A question pokes and prods that which has not yet been poked and prodded

? A question wants a playmate.

Questions help you do

If you can develop your questioning skills you will immediately begin to expand your options, you will have more alternatives, you will generate extra possibilities, you will have more choices. All these things will lead you into action, to Do things.

Your new questioning skills will enable you to become less of a knower and more of a doer. You will annoy authorities and astound your friends. This alone, can be a good enough reason to ask more questions.

Do it bad!

My friend, Leslie Buckland, was President of Caribiner Inc. in New York, the world's largest producer of business meetings. Leslie often used to say, 'If something is worth doing it's worth doing badly.' Why? Doesn't this seem a contradiction for a man who was known internationally for setting the standard of quality in business meetings?

Caribiner can go into a hotel ballroom anywhere in the world, turn it into a circus or a theatre in 24 hours and stage, for one performance only, the business equivalent of a Broadway show – original music, dancers, actors, fireworks, etc. – then 24 hours later, strike the set, leaving it as they found it. They stage multi-million dollar productions all over the world for companies like IBM, McDonald's, and Mercedes-Benz, where quality is the absolute key. Yet Les often says, 'If something is worth doing, it's worth doing badly'. *Why?*

Bad can lead to good

This is the paradox of action, of decision-making, of getting things done. The mistake-phobiacs are so afraid of doing something badly they get nothing done at all! 'Our doubts', said William Shakespeare, 'are traitors and make us lose the good we oft might win by fearing to attempt.'

Very often there's no 'right way' to do things. Les, and other people of action, like trauma surgeons or astronauts, know that one has to get started and do something, get the process moving.

Even if you make a mistake or do it badly, get going. You can always change things, make adjustments and corrections. You can make it work and make it work well, but first you have to get it up and running. Bad can always be changed to good. Sitting back and waiting for perfection often means inertia and failure.

Using questions

For an experiment (that is, to try out and see what happens) try asking questions like these:

? How does this company make a profit?

? When you swim, how do you breathe?

? Why does this shop close at 6pm?

? Can I work longer hours?

? Why was my request refused?

? Can I have a money-back guarantee? Why not?

? Why shouldn't I be with someone I like?

? What's so good about always being busy?

? What are my skills?

? What is your authority? Why?

? What is missing here? What else?

? How are board members selected?

? What determines the number of directors on the board?

? How was this decision made? Why?

? Why is this rule necessary? Can it be improved?

? Am I needed here?

? How can this be more fun?

One Question Two Question

If you were given the opportunity to ask anyone in the world today just one question:

1. What would be the question? and
2. Of whom would you ask it?

If you were given the opportunity to ask anyone in history whoever lived just one question:

1. What would be the question? and
2. Of whom, in all of history, would you ask your question?

14

NOTICE

AS MENTIONED BEFORE, cognetics comes from the words, 'cognitive cybernetics'. Cognitive, of course, means to do with 'thinking' and cybernetics means to do with 'feedback'. In other words, cognetics is thinking based on feedback. The reason you think is so that you can notice the feedback created by your thinking and action. This feedback then becomes the stimulus for further thinking. Thinking...Feedback...Thinking, etc.

Objectivity

The basis of all science is observation and measurement – noticing things. A clever brainuser is a clever noticer and a clever noticer is objective. The skill of noticing is objectivity. Detachment is also important in noticing things. With detachment you can have a broader, clearer view of the situation.

For example, when pouring a glass of champagne you notice feedback. You notice when the champagne level is nearing the top of the glass and so you begin to stop pouring. If you didn't notice this then you might continue pouring and the whole system runs out of control.

In fact, noticing things is the basis of controlling things. This champagne situation is an example of a 'feedback system'. Noticing and measuring feedback in systems in order to control those systems is what cybernetics is all about. Noticing this feedback created by your thinking, in order to control it, is what cognitive cybernetics or cognetics is all about.

Cybernetics

During World War II, Dr Norbert Weiner, Professor of Mathematics at MIT – Massachusetts Institute of Technology – invented cybernetics, as a body of mathematics to help anti-aircraft technology and also to help our understanding of mental acts via formal systems analysis.

The main problem with an airplane as a target was that it moved. Cybernetics worked by noticing the 'degree of miss' between an ack-ack shell and the airplane target and feeding back that information to the weapon so that an immediate adjustment could be made and then another shell fired.

This loop would be quickly repeated many times allowing the weapon to 'educate itself' and close in on its target. This gave the weapon its characteristic ack-ack-ack-ack-ack-ack-ack firing sequence. Fire... feedback... fire... feedback... fire... feedback... fire... feedback... fire... feedback... fire... feedback, etc., until it closed in on its target.

Feedback loops

This kind of technology, as with many other advances, has been largely developed by military scientists. Missiles work the same way, wiggling to their target by using heat sensors to locate the target's engine and noticing the feedback in order to make a rudder or rocket adjustment. Noticing the feedback in the central activity that allows the missile to reach its goal. The Patriot missiles used in Iraq show how this technology has been developed to such an extraordinary degree by the US Star Wars project. The Patriot's ability to catch Scud missiles in the air is roughly equivalent to you driving along at 70 mph and plucking a single blade of grass, previously painted red, as you go by.

This kind of advanced Star Wars cybernetics technology may be used in the future to shield planet earth from meteors which are an increasing worry to scientists. Meteors remain just as serious a threat to life on the planet today as they were to our Jurassic ancestors.

Cybernetics is all about servo-mechanisms, goal-seeking behaviour, feedback loops, positive and negative feedback systems, self-stabilising systems, homeostasis and the control of systems, and how they might apply to biological or mechanical systems.

THINKING... FEEDBACK... THINKING... FEEDBACK ...
THINKING... FEEDBACK... THINKING... FEEDBACK ...
THINKING... FEEDBACK... THINKING... FEEDBACK ...
THINKING... FEEDBACK... THINKING... FEEDBACK ...
THINKING... FEEDBACK... THINKING...

Edward de Bono

Although popularly known for his invention of the term 'lateral thinking', now in the Oxford Dictionary, Dr Edward de Bono's greatest contribution is that written up in his book *The Mechanism of Mind*.

De Bono follows on from MIT Professor Norbert Wiener's idea that the brain must be an information-processing machine and the way it 'minds' should be capable of being expressed in informational terms.

The brain as a body system

Dr de Bono was Professor of Investigative Medicine at Cambridge. He was an expert in body systems. In *The Mechanism of Mind*, which he wrote 28 years ago, Edward de Bono builds a model of how the brain, as an organ of the body, is very likely to operate as mind.

This model shows how the brain, by operating along the lines of other body systems like the liver system or lung system, can produce a mind, a biological system to process information. By showing how the brain operates as a self-organising, patterning system, de Bono saw the need to promote lateral thinking as a compensation mechanism for some of the limitations of the brain/mind patterning system.

Cognetics

Cognitive cybernetics – cognetics – is about the practical application of cybernetics in cognitive science, which is the science of information-processing in animals and machines.

In the Western world we are historically more concerned with judgement than with movement. We are more concerned with 'rightness' than with effectiveness. Other cultures, for instance Japan, are more concerned with the PROCESS than the result.

This often gives them a big advantage over us. Effectiveness is reaching an alternating balance between thought-based action and action-based thought. Thinking... Feedback... Thinking... Feedback... Thinking... Feedback... Thinking... Feedback... Thinking..., etc.

As an experiment try pouring a glass of wine without getting any feedback, with your eyes closed. What happened? How else can you get feedback even with your eyes closed?

Power to the People, power to the Customer

George Gallup founded the Gallup Poll at Princeton, New Jersey, which became the world's first system to objectively and scientifically measure – that is, to notice – public and customer opinion. He was also the inventor of market research and the ultimate saviour of the customer. The very existence of the Gallup Poll has changed forever the future of the human race. The Gallup Poll makes it increasingly difficult for individuals to claim 'I-am-right', to claim they alone 'know what's best' for the public now that accurate scientific measurement of the public/customer viewpoint is possible.

As the inventor of market research and the Gallup Poll, Professor Gallup has so empowered the public viewpoint that I believe his invention may be the greatest act of democracy ever performed by any scientist.

His research covered the fields of: Health; Religion; Politics; Journalism; Advertising; Entertainment; Business; Education and Human Thinking. It can be said that no other person in history has ever had the opportunity to notice and record the views of so many humans on so many aspects of their existence, and in so many parts of their world!

Teaching Thinking

A lesser known side of Dr Gallup was his interest in humans and the factors which influence their opinions, attitudes, thinking and aspirations. He once told me, teaching people to think for themselves was the most important thing in the world to do.

Bom in Jefferson, Iowa, in 1900, he attended the University of Iowa and spent ten years as a teacher there and at Drake, Northwestern and Columbia universities. He had a strong interest in education and what could be done to improve it. He had more than ten honorary Doctorate Degrees from colleges and universities around the world. George died at his Switzerland home in 1984.

Notice the CVS

As my mentor, Professor Gallup helped with the design of cognetics by impressing upon me the need to measure or notice the CVS (Current View of the Situation) as a basis for moving to the BVS (Better View of the Situation). We will explore this further in coming chapters.

Dr Gallup's work, along with that of Weiner, de Bono and others, stands as one of the first great examples of the practical application of the new field of cognitive science.

Your own Gallup Poll question

It can cost around $US20,000 to have a Gallup Poll conducted on just one question. If you could have a Gallup Poll conducted, what one question would you ask? Why would you ask this question?

How to notice things

The main point about noticing is this: try to notice those things that you have NOT YET noticed.

It's easy to notice the information that supports our CVS, our Current View of the Situation. It's difficult to notice the information that falls outside our CVS and so that's exactly why and where we must make a deliberate attempt to notice things.

Opposite Direction

Suppose you're looking north. Once you become aware of the fact, once you notice it, then you can deliberately choose to look south. Looking in the opposite direction is one place to notice things. Try looking in directions that you are not yet looking in. Where are you looking now? Where could you be looking now?

Mistakes

Mistakes are a useful thing to notice. Mistake-phobiacs are so afraid of mistakes that they can't bear to notice them. They can't see that a mistake is an opportunity to make an appropriate adjustment. They can't cope with mistakes Mistake-phobiacs are always 'right'. 'Nothing is more dangerous than the certainty that one is right', writes Francois Jacob, winner of the Nobel Prize for Medicine:

> 'Nothing is potentially so destructive as the obsession with a truth one considers absolute. All crimes in history have been the result of fanaticism of one type or another. All massacres have been carried out in the name of virtue, of true religion, of legitimate nationalism, of proper policy, of right ideology: in short, in the name of the fight against somebody else's truth. '
>
> The Logic of Life (Penguin 1989)

It's important to be able to notice mistakes in order to be able to correct them and move on. (OK, move on.) To do this effectively one needs to be objective rather than destructive, to be creative rather than judgemental. Try noticing mistakes that you have not yet noticed. Correct them and move on. 'Failure is only the opportunity to more intelligently begin again', said Henry Ford.

Future consequences

Future consequences can be the most difficult things to notice especially in advance, which is one of the best times to notice them. This is a bit of a paradox. How can we notice a consequence that has not yet happened? How can we notice the future?

Actually we do it every time we ride a skateboard, apply make-up or use a chainsaw. By noticing potential consequences we can avoid them in advance, if we wish. The most difficult consequences to notice in advance are the long-term ones. If I do such-and-such what will happen in 10 years? In 20 years?

As the many possible futures hurtle towards us at an ever-increasing rate we will have to get better and better at noticing long-term consequences so that we can choose the future we want to be in.

Last chance to choose a safe future

We are currently destroying the world's forests at the rate of an acre per second. In 10 years, most of the earth's oxygen producing forests will be gone, if we don't notice the long-term consequences and make some big changes.

We have already destroyed three-quarters of Australia's tropical rainforests and about two-thirds of the rest of our forests. We have made a hole in our protective ozone layer already the size of Mount Everest.

Canadian scientist David Suzuki, Professor of Genetics at the University of British Columbia, says, 'We are the last generation who

will have any say on the future of our planet because after our lifetime it will all be gone.' If we are to make the necessary adjustments to our current behaviour, to ensure a safe future, we will have to get much better at noticing the future consequences of our current behaviour. Try noticing future consequences that you have not yet noticed.

Why notice things?

What would happen if you didn't notice things? Usually when we don't notice something we make a mistake. When we don't notice the mistake, we make another mistake. And so on. However, when we do notice the mistake, then we can adapt to adjust in some way and then proceed. START – DO – NOTICE – THINK. - SDNT - SDNT.

Input

'You have two ears and one mouth so use them in that proportion' – so the saying goes. And yes, ears are certainly good for input, for noticing. Eyes come in handy. The tongue and the nose work well together. And, an assortment of fingers and toes play their part. We do have around five input senses we are told, and these are all useful for noticing. Our experience, patterns built up over the years, can help us to notice things; and, of course, they can also hinder us in noticing things.

Habits of noticing

We can use repetition to develop special habits of noticing. In a room, a carpenter habitually notices wooden things and how poorly, or otherwise, they are made. A businessman notices business opportunities in a situation. A lawyer notices loopholes, a soldier notices... What does a soldier notice?

Skill and training

Actually, the first time I was formally taught to expand my noticing skills was in my army infantry training. In those Vietnam days, we were taught how to notice things in the jungle that we hadn't yet noticed.

Shape, shine, silhouette, size, sound (I still remember). Through practice drills and field exercises we were taught to notice booby traps, thin wires, panji pits and the other hidden delights of jungle warfare not noticeable to the untrained civilian eye. We were taught to expand our range of vision from around 90 degrees to 180 degrees. We were taught to notice things at night – night vision.

How many input ports does your necktop have? How well do you notice things? How well could you notice things? What did you do today to increase your noticing skills? What will you do tomorrow to increase your noticing skills? Does it matter? Why?

Distractions

Sometimes we don't notice things because we become distracted. Magicians use this principle so you won't notice how they do their magic tricks. But sometimes we become distracted for other reasons. Here are ten ways you can deal with distractions:

1. Yield to them then send them on their way

2. Breathe them out - relax, take a deep breath and slowly exhale imagining the distraction to be leaving your body as you breathe out.

3. Ignore the distraction

4. Concentrate on emptying your mind, either with a broom or removing the distraction with a vacuum cleaner.

5. Say NO to the distraction.

6. Say YES to the distraction and let it become the new focus of your attention.

7. Visualise your mind like a blackboard where the distraction is chalked. Now, wipe it clean.

8. Imagine collecting up any distractions in your hand, crumple them and then throw them away.

9. Imagine tossing the distraction into a fast-flowing stream and let them be carried off.

10. If necessary, you can try several combinations of these suggestions.

Brain training

We all have blind spots - those areas that we habitually have difficulty in seeing or noticing.

What is one of your own most important blind spots?

✎ ....

Why do you think you have your blind spot?

✎..

What have been some of the consequences for you as a result of your blind spot?

✎..

15

THINK

WHAT IS THINKING? This question could keep a room full of philosophers happy for a hundred years. But in the School of Thinking we are not concerned with thinking as contemplation, philosophical discussion or academic description, we are concerned with thinking as an operating skill – the kind of thinking that gets things done. The definition we use is: *Thinking is the skill of using intelligence to get things done.*

Thinking vs Doing?

To many people THINKING is the opposite of DOING. They set these two activities up as mutually-exclusive opposites in their mind. With practice, however, you can develop your ability to use thinking as a skill, just like you can develop cooking, golf, leadership, painting, acting or aikido. All human skills can be learned or developed.

Paul MacCready, inventor of the Gossamer Albatross and the father of man-powered flight, once wrote to me from California:

'When first watching a School of Thinking class in action, I was amazed that something so simple and so much fun could be so quick and effective in developing a person's 'thinking muscle'. We all as individuals and as caretakers of our precious earth, need these thinking skills'.

Dr MacCready's metaphor of thinking as a 'muscle' is a good one. It's better than the old-fashioned idea of thinking as a 'gift'. If thinking is only a gift, there's not much you can do about it. But if it's more like a muscle then there's a lot you can do to develop your thinking power.

That's why we look at thinking as a skill. We want to help you enhance your skill and develop your intellectual capital. The goal is to reach an alternating balance between thought-based action and action-based thought.

Thought-based action: THINK – START – DO

Thought-based action is the kind of action that's based on thinking. For example, you are reading a magazine and you read a story set in the Greek island of Patmos. You start to think about the Greek islands and decide you want to actually go there.

You figure out a plan, you find out about costs for fares, etc., you set a date and you finally go and visit Patmos and the Greek islands. You thought something out, got started and then did it. Thought-based action: THINK – START – DO. This is how I came to visit Patmos in the summer of '84.

Action-based thought: DO – NOTICE – THINK

Action-based thought is the kind of thinking that's based on action. For example, a customer walks into a store and the salesperson says 'Can I help you?'. The customer immediately says, 'No thanks, just looking' then pirouettes and walks out of the store. Most salespeople keep making the same mistake day-after-day, week-after-week, year-after-year.

But the thinking salesperson might say to him/herself something like: 'Whenever a customer walks into the store and I ask if I can help them I notice that usually drives them back out of the store. Maybe I can think of some other thing I could do that would not have that effect. What could I do instead?' Action-based thought: DO – NOTICE – THINK.

The alternating balance

The skilled thinker can alternate the balance between thought-based action and action-based thought, between THINK – START – DO and DO – NOTICE – THINK. This is what cognetics is all about – action based on noticing feedback, and feedback based on noticing action: SDNT = START – DO – NOTICE – THINK continuing in a continuous series of loops or a kind of cognetics spiral on into the future, exploring the cognos, the vast universe of possible thoughts.

The cognetics spiral

START DO NOTICE THINK
START DO NOTICE THINK
START DO NOTICE THINK
START DO NOTICE THINK
START DO NOTICE THINK
START DO NOTICE THINK
START DO NOTICE THINK

...spiralling on into the cognos.

Start Do Notice Think, or its trigger code SDNT, is a powerful search-engine for your necktop that will enable the brainuser to approach any situation, any problem, any opportunity with confidence. To be doubly negative, there is no situation that can't be managed by SDNT:

1. First you Start. This is like switching the necktop from OFF to ON.

2. Then you Do... something... anything.

3. Then you Notice the feedback from your actions, carefully and objectively.

4. Then you Think. What happened? What were the consequences? What did I like about them? What didn't like about them?

5. Then repeat 1 to 5.

This is exploring, and off you go again... SDNT SDNT SDN' SDNT SDNT SDNT SDNT SDNT SDNT SDNT SDNT SDNT SDNT SDNT SDNT SDNT SDNT SDNT... on into the future, surfing the cognos.

What if...? thinking

One of the most famous users of the 'what if ...?' type of thinking was a young thinker, a lad of sixteen, called Albert Einstein. At that age Albert wrote to his uncle wondering what he would see if he was sitting on a light beam.

By the time he was 26, in 1905, he had solved that problem and changed forever the laws of physics and the way future generations would understand the world. This 'what if ...? thinking he called a *gedanken* or 'thought experiment'. One of the great thinker's most quoted sayings is, *'Imagination is more important than knowledge.'*

Science acknowledges Einstein's thought experiments as among the greatest triumphs ever produced by a human brain His thinking feats made him famous, not just in the scientific community, but amongst the public at large. He, in effect, became science's first superstar! Until he died in 1955 he was always at the centre of much publicity and public interest.

No socks

At first Einstein was the eccentric, the genius who never wore socks Then he became a leading pacifist and opponent of rearmament whose traditional education left him with a lifelong suspicion of all forms of authority. As the Nazis spread across Europe he advised

President Roosevelt that it would be possible to make an atom bomb. However, when the bombs were actually used on Japan he immediately sought the establishment of a world authority that would control these weapons.

Today, posters of Albert Einstein are bestsellers. It's encouraging to know that these posters of the scientist, humanitarian, inventor, Nobel Prize winner and thinker, are stuck on the walls of many a teenager's bedroom along with their other heroes of rock, movies and sport.

Hardware and software

Like Einstein, we all have some pretty awesome hardware in our twin-hemispheric, necktop, personal computer. Our problem, however, is that we are very short on software. The traditional Western approach to thinking is simply reactive, logical judgement-the slapping on of the 'right' and 'wrong' labels.

This has always led to extravagant, destructive clashes throughout history and is hopelessly inadequate for designing a safe future in a rapidly changing world. In this book you can go beyond your existing logic software with new software called cognetics.

Logic and Cognetics

If you would like to get a 'feel' for the difference between logic and cognetics (both of which are software systems designed to handle information in the brain) you can try the following simple exercise:

There follow two sets of words which help describe the process involved in each brain software – logic or cognetics. Relax for a moment and take a nice deep breath, then repeat the words in capitals slowly and evenly over and over until you get the 'feel' for the way each software handles its information. You may have noticed that logic uses a kind of labelling or 'mail-sorting' approach to dealing with information.

Exercise

DO IT FIRST FOR LOGIC (REPEAT ABOUT 10 TIMES):

RIGHT ..... WRONG

RIGHT ..... WRONG

RIGHT ..... WRONG

RIGHT ..... WRONG

RIGHT ..... WRONG

RIGHT ..... WRONG

RIGHT ..... WRONG

RIGHT ..... WRONG

RIGHT ..... WRONG

RIGHT ..... WRONG

DO IT NOW FOR COGNETICS (REPEAT ABOUT 10 TIMES):

START ..... DO ..... NOTICE ..... THINK

START ..... DO ..... NOTICE ..... THINK

START ..... DO ..... NOTICE ..... THINK

START ..... DO ..... NOTICE ..... THINK

START ..... DO ..... NOTICE ..... THINK

START ..... DO ..... NOTICE ..... THINK

START ..... DO ..... NOTICE ..... THINK

START ..... DO ..... NOTICE ..... THINK

START ..... DO ..... NOTICE ..... THINK

START ..... DO ..... NOTICE ..... THINK

Logic reacts to information using judgement based on historical experience:-

It fits, it's right; it doesn't fit, it's wrong, etc.

This is, of course, very useful in a secondary way and for looking back at static, theoretical situations. By itself, however, it's totally inadequate for dealing with most fluid, forward-looking situations in real life.

With cognetics, you may have noticed a quite different, open-ended, spiralling effect as movement is created (START... DO) and then feedback is evaluated (NOTICE... THINK) and further movement, with adjustments based on the feedback, is then continued.

Thinking is movement

There is no 'right' way to think. The key to thinking is movement. Movement through the cognos, movement through think-space, movement through the ideosphere, movement through the universe of possible thoughts.

Whether you move out or in or up or down, sideways, backwards or upside-down, reverse pikes, it doesn't matter. Whether you take great leaps, use stepping-stones, random provocations, lateral thinking, flip-a-coin, or fantastic images, it all works.

Whether you use intuition, alpha-visualisations, TM, tarot cards, I-Ching, runes, prayer, auto-suggestion, cognetics, hypotheticals, scientific method, professional counselling, net surfing or 'ask the oracle'– it all adds up to movement.

The essential key in thinking is movement – escape from your CVS. Once you have movement, you get feedback and, as we have seen, it's this noticing feedback which is the essential ingredient for further thinking, which is to say, surfing the cognos.

Thought experiment

A Thought Experiment is an experiment you carry out in your brain, using only thinking – your imagination. For example, you could imagine what would happen if cigarettes were square and not round. You think it through and imagine the consequences and possibilities and outcomes.

Brain training

- Design your own THOUGHT EXPERIMENT.

- Explain your THOUGHT EXPERIMENT to an associate and discuss at least three of the imagined outcomes.

SDNT SDNT SDNT SDNT
SDNT SDNT SDNT SDNT
SDNT SDNT SDNT SDNT
SDNT SDNT SDNT SDNT
SDNT SDNT SDNT SDNT
SDNT SDNT SDNT SDNT
SDNT SDNT SDNT SDNT
SDNT SDNT SDNT SDNT
SDNT SDNT SDNT SDNT
SDNT SDNT SDNT SDNT
SDNT SDNT SDNT SDNT
SDNT SDNT SDNT SDNT
SDNT SDNT SDNT SDNT
SDNT SDNT SDNT SDNT
SDNT SDNT SDNT SDNT
SDNT SDNT SDNT SDNT

CVSTOBVS

Cognetics Operating System™

CURRENT VIEW SITUATION TO BETTER VIEW SITUATION
CURRENT VIEW SITUATION TO BETTER VIEW SITUATION
CURRENT VIEW SITUATION TO BETTER VIEW SITUATION
CURRENT VIEW SITUATION TO BETTER VIEW SITUATION
CURRENT VIEW SITUATION TO BETTER VIEW SITUATION
CURRENT VIEW SITUATION TO BETTER VIEW SITUATION
CURRENT VIEW SITUATION TO BETTER VIEW SITUATION
CURRENT VIEW SITUATION TO BETTER VIEW SITUATION
CURRENT VIEW SITUATION TO BETTER VIEW SITUATION
CURRENT VIEW SITUATION TO BETTER VIEW SITUATION
CURRENT VIEW SITUATION TO BETTER VIEW SITUATION
CURRENT VIEW SITUATION TO BETTER VIEW SITUATION
CURRENT VIEW SITUATION TO BETTER VIEW SITUATION
CURRENT VIEW SITUATION TO BETTER VIEW SITUATION
CURRENT VIEW SITUATION TO BETTER VIEW SITUATION
CURRENT VIEW SITUATION TO BETTER VIEW SITUATION
CURRENT VIEW SITUATION TO BETTER VIEW SITUATION
CURRENT VIEW SITUATION TO BETTER VIEW SITUATION
CURRENT VIEW SITUATION TO BETTER VIEW SITUATION
CURRENT VIEW SITUATION TO BETTER VIEW SITUATION
CURRENT VIEW SITUATION TO BETTER VIEW SITUATION
CURRENT VIEW SITUATION TO BETTER VIEW SITUATION
CURRENT VIEW SITUATION TO BETTER VIEW SITUATION
CURRENT VIEW SITUATION TO BETTER VIEW SITUATION

16

CVS≠BVS

'I would love to have a management team that really under-stood the CVSTOBVS equation. It's the value-added role in the management process

Jack Welch, Chairman, General Electric

The Cognetics Operating System, represented by the code CVSTOBVS, is the premium software in this book. It is also the most powerful: necessarily so, because it enables the brainuser to upgrade from logic, the existing primary thinking software, and to allow logic to take its useful place as a secondary software package.

CVSTOBVS is a perception switch. It allows the brainuser to think outside the square. It enables you to switch cognitive patterns on command – from Current View Situation (CVS) to Better View Situation (BVS). (Hence, CVS-to-BVS.) It is also your main antidote to the Plato Truth virus. It is based on the Law of Cognetics.

Beyond logic

500 years ago Columbus set sail. The Talavera Commission reported to Queen Isabella on Columbus' idea – to reach Japan in the East by sailing West and to discover other lands en route – that the adventure was 'uncertain and impossible to any educated person.'

They told the queen that the proposed voyage would take three years. Even if the ships could return, which was highly unlikely, the Commission reported it would be a wasted expedition, 'For God would surely not have allowed any uninhabited land of real value to be concealed from His people for so many centuries.'

The experts scorned his project. But Columbus did set sail. Thirty-three days later he discovered half the world! I have always thought that Columbus was a very clever brainuser.

Unique rightness

Based solely on their accumulated experience, the experts pointed out that the Admiral's mission was hardly a logical one because his mathematics were wrong. So if his mathematics were wrong, therefore Columbus was wrong. They were convinced of the soundness of their logic.

Yet if all our thinking and actions were based only on the 'unique rightness' of our own experience, then progress would be slow or impossible. There could be no room for insight, quantum leaps, outside-the-square-thinking, or the Eureka phenomenon. There could be no room for humour. There could be no room for humility.

Sometimes experts use their experience not to explore the future, but merely to protect the past. Many an expert arrives at a situation and forms an instant judgement. This is based on his unique background, his personal expectations, his values, his mood, his agenda and other factors.

He sees things in a certain way and makes a snap judgement based on his current perceptions. If he is using logic as his main cognitive operating system, the expert often uses his expertise, not as a basis to explore the situation, but merely to back-up and support his snap judgement, and to keep himself 'right'. It seems that the more expert thinkers are, the better they are able to defend their point of view. They get trapped in it by their own expertise. They cannot escape their CVS, their Current View of the Situation.

Now I know this never happens to you, dear brainuser (wink, wink!) but you've probably seen other people fall into this hole. It's a very dangerous one to fall into.

The thinker, the clever brainuser, might take a different approach to a proposition presented to them. They would use their experience, whether thin or quite formidable, to provide an information basis for exploring the idea. They may notice what they think is good about it, and what they think is bad about it. Then, they may deliberately set out to notice how it could be improved, perhaps to lead to an even better idea, a Better View of the Situation.

To help you do this we use a little switch called CVS-TO-BVS. The switch is simply a neuroware device for programming cognetics into your short-term memory.

It takes just one second to use this switch, to say CVS-TO-BVS. If you practise this switch for ten days it will become a habit and a permanent piece of neuroware in your necktop. After ten days, you'll have it forever.

The law of cognetics

The Law of Cognetics is:

> THE CURRENT VIEW OF THE SITUATION (CVS)
> CAN NEVER BE EQUAL TO
> THE BETTER VIEW OF THE SITUATION (BVS).

Just think about that for ten seconds. See if it makes any sense to you and whether you can embrace the law or whether you can't. Say it to yourself out loud and see how you react to it: Do you have any trouble with this law? This is really the most important law for thinking. The more you can bring conviction into this, the more it will work for you.

To simplify this you say:-

> CVS CAN NEVER BE EQUAL TO BVS
> CVS≠BVS

Antidote to PTV

This law – CVS ≠ BVS – is a strong antidote to PTV and I will show you how to exploit it and put it to use in the next chapter. As I continue to design ways to neutralise PTV I prefer to use the tools of science. Why? What is it that makes science so unique? What is it that separates the scientific approach to matters from other non-scientific approaches? The answer is: testing and measuring.

It's only by putting a theory up against testing and measuring that we can move it from science-fiction towards science-fact. I say towards because we can never actually prove anything in science in an absolute sense.

What we say is that after testing and measurement of the evidence, the 'balance of evidence' as it now stands would indicate that such-and-such a theory seems valid. It's a 'more likely truth'. This always gets updated at a later stage by other scientists as testing and measuring procedures improve and as new theories, new 'more likely truths', are put forward.

Not testing and measuring = faith

The absence of testing and measuring is: faith. When we are in a non-scientific mode we can use faith as a way of coming to a point of view. There are many things in human culture that don't lend themselves very well to testing and measuring and some people still get value out of believing in them.

For example, there exists a myriad of myths and legends, folklore, superstitions and fortune-telling – some of which turn out on scientific analysis to have a basis in fact – plus a rich collection of metaphysical beliefs. These have provided a great deal of interest and support to millions of people even though such belief systems elude any form of objective testing or measurement.

For example, no-one has ever been able to test or measure the existence of 'Guardian Angels'. So this is an unscientific belief that can be simply accepted on faith if one chooses to do so.

Some people live their lives on the principle that they are somehow 'protected' and cite instances in which they have been helped to make better decisions by a power they perceive outside 'themselves'. Others may find the concept unwelcome; a spiritual Big Brother following them around can seem an infringement of personal liberty. A few people actually 'see' angels and talk to them personally. Books are available that tell you how to do this.

Belief systems

Although most of the world's total population of 6 billion do not actively support a religion of any kind, it was recently estimated by a religious leader that a large minority, around 30 per cent, still hope to get value and comfort out of religious beliefs of one kind or another.

Most of these believers were born into major world religions like Judaism, Christianity, Islam, Hinduism or Buddhism which are split into thousands of sub-groups with a range of variations in their beliefs and customs.

In addition, there is a staggering range of smaller religious cults and belief systems of a variety which testifies to the richness and diversity of human imagination.

These belief systems require believers to take a leap of faith and to believe in things that we may not be able to test or measure. These religious beliefs fall outside the scientific method. This doesn't necessarily mean their claims are not true or their mysteries didn't happen, it simply means that the balance of evidence is so slim that we have no way of knowing whether they are true; and so, if we accept them, we do so by taking a leap of faith.

Many people are quite able to take such a leap of faith. Many others may have had a set of beliefs culturally programmed into their brain when they were very small children.

To be considered scientifically valid, however, a proposition must be able to be tested or measured independently. It is not enough to simply measure the number of people who believe it. Just because a million people believe the earth is flat is not enough to make it flat. If a million becomes ten million the earth will still not lose its third dimension.

Laws of Moses

Sometimes we believe things we are told to believe just because we never really thought the matter through ourselves. It may simply be an area that has been protected from thinking for many years.

For example, Moses was a leader of ancient times and, like all leaders, he needed his people to adhere to his laws. He said that his ten laws or commandments should be obeyed. The reason that they should be obeyed, he claimed, is because they were given to him, privately, on a mountain, by his god, Yahweh.

By making this claim, Moses positioned these laws with the highest possible authority. They were not his laws, said Moses, but God's laws. This is a very old story that many people just accept but have never really updated or thought through for themselves.

If you do stop to think about this story in the light of what we know today you may be able to ask yourself for a more plausible version. Since there were no witnesses or evidence of any kind we don't know whether Moses' version actually happened or not.

However, millions of people who adhere to the Judeo-Christian tradition have simply chosen to take a leap of faith and to believe Moses' claim. A Christian or Jewish scientist could not accept this story as a scientist, but could accept it, by a leap of faith, as part of their religious belief system. One of me must be right!

Believing science and believing faith

The argument between science and religion is a false one. It is simply a matter of distinguishing between those things we believe because we have tested them until they are part of science, and those things we believe because we cannot test them so we take a leap of faith.

There is no reason why we cannot hold viewpoints in both areas as long as we are able to distinguish between the two.

Your beliefs

If you wish, you can explore some of your own beliefs, whether about your religion, your job and career or your future.

Ten Things That I Believe (But Cannot Prove):-

1. About my religion, I believe ...

2. About my religion, I believe ...

3. About my religion, I believe ...

4. About my job, I believe ...

5. About my job, I believe ...

6. About my job, I believe ...

7. About my future, I believe ...

8. About my future, I believe ...

9. About my future, I believe ...

10. About my beliefs, I believe ...

Thought experiment:

Try to conduct a thought experiment. In your mental laboratory, try to use your thinking skill to generate an alternative explanation to Moses' story and perhaps tell me what you have come up with. Since it is only an experiment you can be as creative as you are capable of being.

Try to do your own experiment before looking at the ones below.

Here are some of the experiments supplied by SOT members. Of course, many of these thinkers come from cultures that do not use the Moses story. This is just a small sample of responses:

- 'An alternative explanation may not involve Moses at all. It is possible that the entire story of Moses was concocted many years after the alleged incident. Myth and legend constitute a large part of all religions, and stories are made up and embellished through repeated tellings. In fact, History is often referred to as 'his story'; *his* referring to the entrenched power or leader of the time.'

- 'Oriental philosophies like Buddhism and yoga tell us (and invite us to verify personally) that there is a deep inner knowledge attainable through meditation and personal effort. Maybe Moses made the effort and had the insights but he felt that most of his people would not make this effort. So, to make it easier for them he used the 'God' idea.'

- 'Moses may have been smoking or eating the leaves of 'The Burning Bush'. Was mescalin around in those days? '

- 'Moses was actually a slider, a time traveller from the future, so he chose to zap back to an alternative (better) future and collect their guidelines for creating a better life. He knew that the people in the time he was returning to would not believe in time travel but would accept 'the word of God' more easily.'

- 'Maybe Moses had schizophrenia. He really believed he had a private phone line to God and that he was the chosen one to lead his people.'

- 'Moses may have been a poet.'

- 'What if Moses was a control freak who lied to make people follow him?'

- 'Well, Moses may have had a lucid dream in which he imagined meeting an aspect of himself. He wanted to be in charge, as that was the manly thing to be, but thought that an expert needed to be called in. His expert was called Yahweh. Can you tell I've been

118

involved in Jungian dream groups too? Then again, maybe Moses had been smoking papyrus...'

- 'I find it hard to even consider there is another explanation because I don't believe that it happened in the first place. But I guess if you need another explanation then I tender the following: Moses went to the local at about 3 o'clock in the afternoon, promising his wife that he would only be an hour. However, he met some of his mates and they got on to the pool table and started to play pool. They kept winning and kept drinking. Before Moses knew it, it was 11.30 at night. Now, he knew that he was going to be in deep trouble with his wife because he was late again (his wife being about 5 stone heavier than him). So he made up this story that on his way home he saw this bright light and met this dude named God who wanted to get rid of these secrets (tablets). Now Moses, never one to walk away from an opportunity, took them as he saw it as a way to get out of a beating by his wife. That's the way the Ten Commandments came into being.'

- 'Some of the kids decided to play a practical joke on good old Moses... Burning bush... voice of God... The ten commandments? Moses saw through it and decided to play a little trick on the rest of the tribe.'

- 'He was really old and suffering from sclerosis or Alzheimers.'

- 'Ever read *Origins of Consciousness in the Breakdown of the Bicameral Mind* by Julian Jaynes? His theory was that three thousand years ago people literally hallucinated 'gods' which told them what to do. They did not think like we do, but merely followed the voices. Moses probably heard the voice of 'god' literally. By the way, this may explain why the brain works in a patterning system. If Jaynes was right, it was designed to simply follow orders. Consciousness is a weird thing that happened when man learned to write and speak in metaphor. '

- 'Moses may have found the tablets, left by a previous civilisation. He may have received them from an alien.'

- '**Kenny:** I'm sorry but could I skip this reply coz I'm a Christian and I don't think it's right to question the Bible. Please reply.'
'**Reply:** Of course you can skip this or any other question if you feel it is not right to answer. May I ask you why you feel a Christian has no right to question the Bible? '
' **Kenny:** Basically, to us Christians, the Bible is our everything. It's sort of an instruction book for us (a book of 'Dos') and all that's stated in it is true (God never lies). So by asking what alternatives I could think of to explain the case, I feel that it's like questioning God's character. '
'**Reply:** Fair enough! '

17

BVS=CVSx10

Testing & measuring

MEASUREMENT IS A very important skill for the brainuser to develop. Let's look at units of measurement. It's very helpful when trying to measure things, to have a unit of measurement. It means you can keep score and then compare one score against another.

For example, the whole metric system uses a number of units of measurement based on the decimal (or 10) system. We have metres, litres, pounds Sterling and grams. So, if you want to measure how far you have to travel to work, you can do so, and the answer may be 10 metres if you work at home or 10 kilometres if you don't.

You can use pounds to figure costs and overheads and to help control them and bring them down. You can also use pounds to figure revenues and sales results and help move them up.

Measuring your job

The more you can bring measurements to aspects of your job the more you can take control and the more interesting your job becomes. What things can you measure in your job?

- Costs – eliminations, reductions or increases?
- Accidents/safety – lower or higher numbers?
- Sales calls – more or less?

- Delivery times – longer or shorter?
- Materials used – more or less?
- Wastage – less or more?
- Industrial disputes – fewer or more often?

Decimal cognetics

In the last chapter, we've already seen that a CVS can never be equal to a BVS. So, what exactly is a BVS?

A BVS is a decimal of a CVS. A CVS is also a decimal of a BVS. In other words, they are related by powers of 10. Sometimes a BVS is 10 times smaller than a CVS. Other times it is 10 times greater. From experience, it is usually the latter, but not always.

By decimalising (yes, it is a word) cognetics we are introducing measurement into the brain software and we get more control. Cognetics now becomes a more useful brain tool. Remember, cognetics is decimal. In cognetics we use the number 10. The deliberate or habitual use of the number 10 is called Tenpower.

BVS=CVSx10

The key to the practical use of this powerful perception switch – CVSTOBVS – is the deliberate effort one makes to try to notice the BVS that is **10 times** better than the CVS.

So, for example, if your CVS is £1 then a BVS might be £10 (or it could be 10p if you owed £1.) If the CVS is on one level, then the BVS can be found on a level **10 times** better than the CVS.

10 times better may be 10 times more, or ten times less, or 10 units forward or 10 units back. It's the deliberate use of tenpower as a provocation to get you to escape from your CVS.

With practice, the '10 times' part of cognetics just becomes easier and easier. This is what tenpower is all about. Remember, mathematically, there are always millions of possible options (literally!) but you must deliberately look for them to see them.

Tenpower helps you to switch patterns of perception. That's all. While it is not important that the number 10 is accurately used, its use is a powerful escape mechanism. Take a leap with tenpower!

Examples:-

- If the CVS is 1 gift, the BVS might be 10 gifts.
- If the CVS is thirst, the BVS might be 10 mouthfuls of water
- If the CVS is 1 e-mail, the BVS might be 10 e-mails.
- If the CVS is 1 step back, the BVS could be 10 steps forward.
- If the CVS is 10 steps forward, the BVS might be 100 steps back.
- If the CVS is red, perhaps the BVS is green.
- If the CVS is up, then the BVS may be down or even much further up.
- If the CVS is to take, the BVS may be to give.
- If the CVS is do it later, the BVS may be do it now.
- If the CVS is 10, the BVS could be 100, or 1.
- If the CVS is 100, the BVS might be 1000, or 10.
- If the CVS is 1, the BVS could be one tenth (or 0.1).
- If the CVS is where you are now, the BVS is to move elsewhere.
- If the CVS is the state we are in, the BVS is a quantum jump to another state, whether 10 times up or 10 times down.

In cognetics, rightness is not as important as movement. Cognetics, using tenpower, enables you to move through information at a rate never before possible with only logic. And, in a rapidly changing world, movement to a better viewpoint is much more important to the thinker than defence of a current viewpoint.

The reason for tenpower is because there are always risks in thinking. It can be risky leaving the safety of a CVS to go out in search of a BVS. But if the rewards are so great, so worthwhile, a true quantum leap, an order of magnitude – then the reward provides its own motivation. You can now have the drive to escape inertia to move towards a BVS.

123

The power of 10

The habitual use of the number 10 gives a very useful measurement and a useful tracking and controlling device for the thinker or clever brainuser. More power, Scotty! Powers of ten are extremely powerful warp-speeds for moving through the cognos, the information universe.

In the unlimited universe of 'thinkspace', powers of ten help us escape from the gravity of our CVS and to move out of orbit and explore the cognos, looking for a BVS.

18

TENPOWER

I WANT TO devote a separate chapter to discussing tenpower, thereby giving it the importance it deserves.

If this was just a book about theory, tenpower could be left out; but it's a book about action. You don't just want to know about cognetics, you also want to be able to DO it.

Practice, repetition, rehearsal

It was revealed to me during my army training lessons, in the late '60s, when I was a 20-year old national serviceman draftee, how amazingly effective was the strategy of REPETITION. Army instructors demonstrated its power by always having us use practice, repetition and rehearsals.

I remember thinking it odd, at the time, that an ambush was actually rehearsed in detail in the field before being laid that night. But why not? Ambushing is a skill and anything that is a skill can be dramatically improved with repetition and practice

A pattern is something that is repeated more often than randomness or chaos. The architecture of a pattern is repetition That's why in a patterning system like the human brain system, repetition is the most powerful learning strategy you can use.

That's also why you'll notice a great deal of repetition in this book. It's not because I've forgotten that I've already discussed something with you. It's to help build patterns in your brain so it becomes easier for you to remember and use the software.

> IN A PATTERNING SYSTEM. LIKE THE HUMAN BRAIN
> SYSTEM. THERE IS NO STRONGER MAGIC THAT CAN BE
> USED THAN THE MAGIC OF REPETITION.

All this is critical when acquiring new skills. And, repeating things ten times is an excellent way to exploit tenpower.

What is tenpower?

Tenpower is the skill of using the powers of ten. Tenpower is a booster mechanism for your brain software. Just like enzymes that boost up chemical reactions or rockets that boost space shuttles, so can tenpower boost your brain software and greatly empower your thinking skills.

Put on a nought!

A nought may not seem like much. If you add it or subtract it from another number, it makes no difference at all. Nought – zero, zilch, nil, nada, nix – barely exists until... you put a nought on the end of another number, and, *mirabile dictu,* that number increases **tenfold!**

That is tenpower! Even the Egyptians had a symbol for tenpower and maybe that's why the pyramids are so big.

In cognetics, thinking is moving through think-space, the information universe, the cognos, by powers of ten. Tenpower can be used in any direction - moving out or moving in.

For example, with tenpower you can move from 1 to 10 to 100 to 1000 to 10000 to 100000 to 1000000 to 10000000, etc.

Or, from 1 to .1 to .01 to .001 to .0001 to .00001 to .000001 to .0000001 and so on.

The habit of tenpower is the habit of using the number ten, the habit of adding a zero or the habit of multiplying by ten. By using tenpower you will equip your necktop with a very powerful booster which will give you an unfair advantage over others when moving through the information environment. The Official Number of the School of Thinking is 10!

Ten repetitions

1. Repetition
2. Repetition
3. Repetition
4. Repetition
5. Repetition
6. Repetition
7. Repetition
8. Repetition
9. Repetition
10. Repetition

Where to use tenpower

You can use tenpower anywhere. There's no 'right' place to use tenpower. Some people use tenpower to get started. Some use tenpower for fitness, practising skills and doing repetitions. You can use tenpower to solve problems, to create opportunities.

Writers can use tenpower to escape writer's block. I use tenpower in teaching thinking skills. Business people use tenpower to plan ahead. Students use tenpower to do the research. Parents use tenpower to help in family discussion Where can you use tenpower?

Why use tenpower?

Putting on a nought is a powerful thing to do. It is the quintessential provocation. Its purpose is to provoke movement through the cognos, to allow you to escape from your present position. It's a bit like using a helicopter.

If you wanted to climb a mountain you might start from the bottom but then when you reach the summit you say, 'Boy, if only we'd come that way it would have been easier'. This is because the view from the top is different from the view at the bottom. If you had a helicopter you could fly to the top first, see the better way, and then go back and use it. (Better doesn't necessarily mean 10 times easier, it depends on what you want from your mountain.)

Quantum leaps and orders of magnitude

Tenpower helps you make quantum leaps in your thinking. It empowers you to escape from the square. It enables you to use orders of magnitude to change your point of view. Then you can use that information if you choose.

Tenpower and Googols

When put on the end of a number, there's no limit to the power of a nought!

How many grains of sand on Sydney's famous Bondi beach? How many raindrops fall in Rio each year? What is the number of words spoken in Washington in a year or even spoken by every American in history?

To cope with questions like these mathematicians need to design very, very large numbers. American mathematician, Edward Krasner has used nought to design his very large number called: the googol.

A googol is a 1 with a hundred noughts put on. A googol looks like this:-

10,000,000,000,000,000,000,000,000,000,000,000,000,000,000,
000,000,000,000,000,000,000,000,000,000,000,000,000,000,000.

How large is a googol? Well, the grains of sand on Bondi beach are about 100,000,000,000,000,000,000 – 1 with twenty zeroes put on.

Much smaller than a googol. Raindrops in Rio are also much smaller than a googol and so are the words of America.

A hundred million atoms placed in a row would only be this long ----, a centimetre. So what about the number of atoms in all of Mt Fuji or even the Alps? No, even they would not make a googol.

Einstein's theories make it possible for astrophysicists to estimate the number of atoms in the whole universe and even that is less than a googol. In fact, a googol is larger than the very largest numbers used in physics and chemistry.

Well, can we provoke a googol? Can we use tenpower on a googol? The answer is, of course, yes. For example, the googolplex is a larger number still: a googol with an extra 10 million, billion noughts put on.

Forgive me if I won't bother to show you what a googolplex looks like, because if I were to try typing out a googolplex by adding noughts to the above googol at the rate of three a second – 000 – and I never stopped to eat or sleep or do anything else, I would be dead and dust long before I got anywhere near it.

Here are ten ways I can use the number 10:

1. I can give ten times more gifts to clients this week than last week.
2. I can send ten times more postcards to friends this month than I did last month.
3. I can call someone who would like to hear from me in ten minutes time.
4. I can consult ten brainusers for their opinion on a matter of importance to me.
5. I can visit ten Web sites that I don't usually visit.
6. I can invite ten people over for a discussion on a matter of importance to all concerned.
7. I can practise a new skill ten times a day for the next 10 days.
8. I can go for a walk in Regent's Park at 10 am.
9. I can cut costs by 10 per cent.
10. I can spend 10 minutes figuring out the first line of the next chapter.

Brain training

What are TEN ways you can use the number 10 over the next ten days?

1. ....

2. ....

3. ....

4. ....

5. ....

6. ....

7. ....

8. ....

9. ....

10. ....

19

CVSTOBVS

ATTENTION! Let's talk about attention. But first, a small experiment:-

> As soon as you have finished reading this sentence, put the book down for a moment, turn your head around 180° and describe something you can see that is coloured green and does not belong to you.
>
> ✎ ....
> ....

OK. Here's the point. Once you look in a direction it's easy to see what is there. Here's how it worked:

1   I gave you the cue to turn your head and look for something specific.
2.   You turned your head and looked.
3.   You saw.

I don't know where you are right now but most readers would have been able to carry this experiment out successfully, once they decided to look. Here's the special insight that I would like you to get now as a result of this little experiment. It will help you get better use out of the brain software. It's this:-

ONCE YOU MOVE YOUR ATTENTION IN A CERTAIN DIRECTION YOU CAN EASILY SEE WHAT THERE IS TO SEE. BUT, THE DECISION TO MOVE YOUR ATTENTION COULD TAKE TWENTY YEARS!

Managing your attention

Many people feel that if there is an opportunity somewhere – a BVS – why, they'll see it and go get it. They assume the very presence of a BVS will make itself known to them, that it will attract their attention. But no, it doesn't work that way. You have to direct your own attention.

BVSs are there all the time, you're tripping over them all day long, literally hundreds of them, but you're not seeing them. The reason you're missing them is obvious: It's impossible to notice a BVS if PTV is holding your attention on defending your CVS.

Attention is the gateway to consciousness. Attention is the business of your mind. Attention is the principal service provided by the management section of your brain which enables you to focus in and have a mind-for you to think about things.

How you move your attention around is very interesting. There are three distinct aspects of attention-directing in your brain:-

1. DISENGAGEMENT: escaping from your present fixation of attention.
2. MOVEMENT: movement of attention across the cognos, the vast universe of possible thoughts.
3. ENGAGEMENT: attending to a new object out of a competition of an infinite multitude of possible candidates.

The CVSTOBVS software is designed as a switch that helps you to control your attention and move it around, especially when your attention is habitually focused on your CVS and its defence. CVSTOBVS can help you disengage and move you attention away from your CVS and to engage it elsewhere on BVS, unless PTV stops you from doing it.

Pay attention! This is a command with which we are a familiar. We all heard it many times as children and we still hear it (if more subtly expressed) every day in business.

We know what it means to direct our attention even though it is something we do inside our head. For example:

- In a noisy cocktail party, you can home in on one particularly interesting conversation.

- In a business presentation, while presenting to the room at large and doing justice to her presentation as planned, an account executive can shift the attention around in her vision to catch the expression on her executive client's face while apparently staring intently at her audio-visual.

- A marketing professional can show you how to deliberately shift your attention away from your product-driven strategy to a better client-driven one and then you can notice the way the information before you rearranges itself.

- A habit of attention may mean that the first thing a hairdresser notices about you is your hair while a dentist may notice your smile instead.

- On arriving at O'Hare International airport, I can pick out my driver from the dozens of others waiting even though my name is badly misspelt on his sign.

- An over-critical, PTV-infected parent can pick out the one mistake in a child's work and not see that the child has accomplished a great deal.

- A shared goal, like Sir Bob Geldof's Band-Aid, can cue a diverse group of individual and even competitive entertainers to give priority to a certain event where otherwise they would all be paying attention to something else.

- A team leader can pull back the attention of her team to a project-in-hand after a distraction has drawn attention away.

- A specific motion put before the board can focus the attention of the directors after a long and wandering discussion.

- Most languages have a word like Achtung! which focuses one's attention sharply.

We experience attention as a filter that the management part of our brain applies to the flood of competing information that comes in from our senses.

Attention disorders

Individuals who have suffered brain-damage can lose their ability to control their attention. Attention disorders are manifested in different ways depending on the nature of the damage. They can take the form of an inability to escape from a particular fixation and so remain stuck in a viewpoint regardless of the demands of ones environment.

Damage to the right side of the brain can make it impossible for patients to pay attention to the side opposite the damaged hemisphere, even to the point of failing to dress the left side of their bodies.

Sometimes, loss of attention-control means constant and debilitating distraction. This is because a person suffering from an attention disorder cannot prevent attention from being diverted by irrelevant stimuli.

The CVSTOBVS switch

Let's now disengage our attention from 'attention' and move it to engage on 'orthogonality'. In quantum physics, where this term originates, orthogonality means mutual exclusivity, that there cannot be two things in the same place at the same time. A switch cannot be both OFF and ON at the same time. If a flipped coin has landed as HEADS, then it cannot also have landed as TAILS at the same time. To get to tails requires at least one more flip of the coin, as anyone who visits a casino for the first time will soon discover.

Switching

Switches are useful because they have at least two positions. This means you can escape from one and move to the other. it only requires a flip of the switch:-

* Switch: HEADS TO TAILS.
* Switch: OFF TO ON.
* Switch: CVS TO BVS.

> CVSTOBVS one hundred times per day
> (CVSTOBVS) × 100pd

Programming the software

So, we wind up with this simple, user-friendly neuro-software package, this powerful thinking switch: from CVS to BVS.

How do we load this neuroware into your necktop? Repetition. Repetition. Repetition... Programming the software switch into your necktop is easy. By exploiting the patterning system of your brain, it's simply a matter of repeating, 'CVS TO BVS'.

You can simply repeat the software code – CVSTOBVS – one hundred times a day. Every day. Starting today!

When I lived on Park Avenue in New York I'd practise by walking along the sidewalk (American for pavement) and as my left foot hit the ground I'd say 'CVS' and as my right foot hit the ground I'd say, '... TO BVS'. CVSTOBVS CVSTOBVS CVSTOBVS CVSTOBVS CVSTOBVS, etc. Not out loud because Bellevue Mental Hospital wasn't far away and they might think I was crazy!

It only takes a second to say 'CVSTOBVS', so 100 repetitions each day takes you 100 seconds or a minute and 40 seconds. That's all. Some do their repetitions in the shower, others while commuting, others combine this brain exercise with exercising their body.

Now what will happen if you do this? It will mean that you're constructing a new executive neurosoftware pattern in your brain. The more you practise, the stronger the pattern. The stronger the pattern, the more power it will have to override PTV.

Instead of finding yourself locked into defending a CVS, you'll hesitate... and you'll look for... and you'll see... and then you'll switch to... a BVS.

And the wonderful thing is that if you paint the pattern strongly enough it will work on every other skill you have. If you practise golf, that won't make you a good cook, will it? Being good at golf doesn't TRANSFER to being a good cook. But cognetics does. It is a process, and as such, it's designed to transfer to any situation whatsoever. It's generic!

Better is clever

You can use cognetics to get better (and 'better' means more clever) at golf, better at cooking, better at studying, better at listening, better at solving business problems, better at selling, better at creating opportunities, better at making decisions, better at handling family matters, better at dealing with personal situations, better at getting better, better at anything!

The first step is to get started on your 100 repetitions each day of CVSTOBVS. To get the full benefit of cognetics, the price is 1 minute and 40 seconds a day! Let's start now. Say this out loud once, it only takes one second. Say: CVSTOBVS. Good. Now let's BVS that. We're going from 1 to 10. That simply means repeating the CVSTOBVS switch ten times. It may feel a little silly at first but no one's going to hurt you for doing it, and you'll already be well on your way.

Say it now ten times out loud:-

CVSTOBVS...CVSTOBVS...CVSTOBVS...CVSTOBVS...CVSTOBVS...
CVSTOBVS...CVSTOBVS...CVSTOBVS...CVSTOBVS...CVSTOBVS...

If you think it's difficult to get you to say it out loud, imagine what it was like to get a Monte Carlo auditorium full of over a thousand IBM executives from all over the world, with five translators, to do it! But they did it, and now they can use it too.

CVSTOBVS simply means that the current way is fine, but there's always a better way, ten times better, if only we remember to deliberately look for it.

If you were to repeat a hundred of those switches each day (that is, repeat CVSTOBVS a hundred times), you would be keeping the switch on in your short-term memory so that the pattern can link up with the projects and situations that come up for you during the day.

For example:

• You might get writer's block while doing a business report – CVSTOBVS

• You might find yourself being a space glutton in a meeting – CVSTOBVS.

• You might be trying to help a customer solve a problem – CVSTOBVS.

• You might be surfing the net looking for an opportunity – CVSTOBVS

• You might be worried and depressed about money – CVSTOBVS.

• You might be about to decide what to have for lunch – CVSTOBVS

• You might be boring a customer– CVSTOBVS

- You might be being bullied by a friend or family member – CVSTOBVS

- You might be watching TV–CVSTOBVS.

Repetition ensures that the switch will pop up at a time when you need to use it. And when it does pop up, then what?

To look is to see

If you decide to look for a BVS,you will see it. Yes, you really will see it. What time is it? (Check your watch and record the time here. Isn't it amazing! The time is always there, BUT you only see it when you actually look for it. Think about that for a moment!) Through training and practice your brain learned (developed the cognitive pattern) to tell the time, long ago. One just needs to use the switch: 'What time is it?'and Hey! Presto! ... we get to see the time! The same applies to a BVS.

It's your attention that controls your behaviour. You need a trigger to manipulate your attention from merely focusing on your CVS and to get it to switch to a BVS. This is also called lateral thinking or creative thinking. You've done it many times before but you need to do it better and much more often – on command!

The key to creativity is remembering to be creative at any particular moment, remembering to use the switch CVSTOBVS. What time is it?

Seek and you shall find

CVSTOBVS will dramatically increase your odds of finding ideas, because you will be actively looking for them, habitually, as a matter of personal policy. You can get a good idea today, a better idea tomorrow and you get the best idea... never! There's always a BVS! This means that you can have a perfectly valid CVS, but there must always be a better one. There's always a BVS!

The difference between the way you use your necktop now and the way it could operate, is up to the software you use Each time you do your 100 repetitions of CVSTOBVS guarantees that you are keeping yourself, your family, your school or company, on the road to a BVS.

And, this software is very cool when it comes to protecting your necktop from PTV.

CVSTOBVS CVSTOBVS
CVSTOBVS CVSTOBVS
CVSTOBVS CVSTOBVS
CVSTOBVS CVSTOBVS
CVSTOBVS CVSTOBVS
CVSTOBVS CVSTOBVS
CVSTOBVS CVSTOBVS
CVSTOBVS CVSTOBVS
CVSTOBVS CVSTOBVS
CVSTOBVS CVSTOBVS
CVSTOBVS CVSTOBVS
CVSTOBVS CVSTOBVS
CVSTOBVS CVSTOBVS
CVSTOBVS CVSTOBVS
CVSTOBVS CVSTOBVS
CVSTOBVS

QRH Styleware™

QUALITY RECOGNITION HUMOUR
QUALITY RECOGNITION HUMOUR
QUALITY RECOGNITION HUMOUR
QUALITY RECOGNITION HUMOUR
QUALITY RECOGNITION HUMOUR
QUALITY RECOGNITION HUMOUR
QUALITY RECOGNITION HUMOUR
QUALITY RECOGNITION HUMOUR
QUALITY RECOGNITION HUMOUR
QUALITY RECOGNITION HUMOUR
QUALITY RECOGNITION HUMOUR
QUALITY RECOGNITION HUMOUR
QUALITY RECOGNITION HUMOUR
QUALITY RECOGNITION HUMOUR
QUALITY RECOGNITION HUMOUR
QUALITY RECOGNITION HUMOUR
QUALITY RECOGNITION HUMOUR

20

QUALITY

STYLEWARE IS new. It's a software package devoted specifically to helping the brainuser choose a world–class style that is compatible with being a PTV-free thinker. When it comes to thinking and behaviour, what can be more important than style?

Style – a strategy for behaviour

A style is a strategy for behaviour. A person's style determines not only what that person will allow him or herself to do but also the way he or she will do it.

Style is that intangible quality about behaviour that leaves a more lasting impression than the behaviour itself. Leaders, like Coco Chanel, Julius Caesar, Pope John XXIII, Princess Diana and the Dalai Lama are remembered as much for their personal style as for their specific actions.

Your personal style

Style provides a framework for daily thinking and daily behaviour. Your personal style shows the way you have positioned yourself in life, reflects your personal life strategy and makes it quite possible to predict the way you are likely to behave in situations.

A loving, gentle woman who treats herself and others with respect is unlikely to begin suddenly and inexplicably behaving like a

Salome. A Scrooge is unlikely to start suddenly playing ball with the kids or donate to Crisis at Christmas – but even a Scrooge can change!

Changing your style

You can't hide your personal style. A single action may or may not go unnoticed but your behaviour patterns are impossible to hide. Repetition attracts attention. Your pattern of behaviour is an exhibition of your personal style just as the pattern of your personal opinions is a loud advertisement of the state of your mind.

But, if you're not happy with your personal style, there is no law that says you have to live with it. You can simply change it. People are doing this every day. Style is a matter of personal choice, once you come of age. It is independent of background, education, or income; it has much to do with thinking – the way you choose to deal with information – in order to deal with situations.

You can choose the personal idiom within which to live your life, just as you can choose the television programmes you wish to watch, the friends you wish to mix with, the clothes you wish to wear, the attitudes you wish to adopt or the Web sites you wish to visit.

Changing is simple once you make the decision. Yet making the decision could take 20 years! It requires an act of will. Not changing, of course, is the decision to keep the style you currently have.

The style of the Clever Brainuser can most readily be described by QRH which stands for the balance among these characteristics: Quality, Recognition, Humour. The QRH style is contemporary and cool but has a taste of what used to be called *noblesse oblige:* the responsibility of power to those less fortunate than oneself.

Your virtual board of directors

When it comes to changing your style, it is very useful to have a clear view of the changes you wish to make and just how you'd like to see yourself. Changing is easier if you have a model or a picture or a coach – someone to give you guidance. For my own guidance, I use my personal group of virtual mentors, my Virtual Board of Directors.

To my Virtual Board (which is happy to meet in my mind whenever I want them to meet) I am free to appoint, as non–executive Director, anyone I choose. I've had members from the present, from the past or from a future not yet a reality. I choose board members for different reasons.

I've had them for speech coaching, for dress, for conversation, for decision–making, for wit, for compassion, for looks, for stimulation, for provocation, for encouragement, for sentimental reasons and for inspiration.

For example, at different times over the years, seats on my Virtual Board have been held by Cicero, Nastassia Kinski, Jean de la Valette, Major Terry Hayes DFC, Julius Caesar, Saki, Audrey Hepburn, Professor George Gallup, W.C. Fields, my father, the Prince of Wales, Richard Dawkins, Dame Elizabeth Murdoch, Fra Martin Luther, Antonio Carlos Jobim, my grandmother, Pope John Paul I, Brian Ferry, Albert Einstein, Oscar Wilde, Professor Roger Short FRS, Musashi Ouee, Queen Isabella and many others whose names I needn't mention.

These have been some of my personal favourites and from whom I have received much advice, support and guidance, free of charge and on–call, anytime, any place. You can operate your Virtual Board along the lines of a thought experiment.

Appointing your directors

The point, of course, is to choose your own Directors because you admire some aspect of their style and you want to emulate that aspect, in your own way, so you need their advice to do so. Other people have told me they use similar strategies and have chosen mental advisers for their own development.

If you wish, you can simply read a good biography of your potential style directors and if it satisfies you, you can appoint them to your board. It's also great fun to do!

Q-quality

When it comes to the subject of style, the clever brainuser is one who always tries to positively upgrade a situation from its current state to a better state. In other words, you are making a deliberate effort to improve the quality of the situation, the quality of the way in which the information is arranged.

Quality is adding value

Quality is important. As a Clever Brainuser you're concerned with adding value to the situation. The point is not whether at any particular moment in time you are successful. What is far more important is the overall style, that is, the deliberate policy of always being concerned with improving the value of the situation – the quest for quality.

Contrast this with the dumb 'whatever–I–can–get–away–with' attitude. Quality is a matter of choice, a matter of style. Only by understanding the process of adding value will we be able to understand the key to productivity and solve what appear to be 'economic' problems.

The habit of quality

Quality is better. Quality is improvement. Quality is general excellence. The habit of quality is the habit of finding a better way, a better possibility, a better view, a better choice, a better alternative, a better outcome, a better attitude, a better opinion, a better life.

If you cannot find a better alternative in a situation then you cannot add value to the situation. That's why CVSTOBVS, the switch to a better way of looking at a situation, is a skill or strategy that is central to the habit of quality. 'Quality is not an act', said Aristotle, 'it's a habit!'

Brainwork

If you were to be quoted on the subject of Quality what would be your Famous Quote?

Make up your own quotable quote on Quality:-

✎ ....

....

Who might have said it?

21

RECOGNITION

Recognition, n. an instance of acknowledging the existence, validity, character and claims of another.
Oxford Dictionary

NO MAN IS an island! You're not Robinson Crusoe! Join the club! What goes around comes around! Live and let live! All for one and one for all! Tit for tat! E Pluribus Unum!

Mammal intelligence is not the only one to discover the strategic benefits of mutual recognition. To make a living, other animals, plants and even bacteria play various games of co-operation and mutual recognition. Mutual recognition is the obvious realisation that what is important to me is also important to you, so let's co-operate.

I'll acknowledge your existence and the matching valid claims that arise and, in return, you'll do the same for me. Mutual recognition. Many people have talked about the value of recognition. It's nothing new. Here are some of them:

Seneca:
'He that does good to another does good also to himself.'

Confucius:
'He who wished to secure the good of others, has already secured his own.'

Hindu Proverb:
> 'Help your brother's boat across, and lo! your own has reached the shore.'

Prof. Richard Dawkins:
> 'Nice guys finish first.'

Western Proverb:
> 'You scratch my back and I'll scratch yours.'

Zig Ziglar:
> 'I believe you can get everything you want in life if you just help enough other people get what they want.'

Marcus Aurelius:
> 'Men exist for the sake of one another.'

Henry Ford:
> 'Coming together is a beginning; Keeping together is a progress; Working together is success.'

Albert Einstein:
> 'Without deep reflection, one knows from daily life that one exists for other people.'

Jesus of Nazareth:
> 'There was a man going from Jerusalem down to Jericho when he fell into the hands of robbers. They stripped him, beat him, and went off leaving him half dead. Now by coincidence a priest was going down that road; when he caught sight of him, he went out of his way to avoid him. In the same way, when a Levite came to the place, he took one look at him and crossed the road. But this Samaritan who was travelling that way came to where he was and was moved to pity at the sight of him. He went up to him and bandaged his wounds, pouring olive oil and wine on them. He hoisted him on to his own animal, brought him to an inn, and

looked after him. The next day he took out two silver coins, which he gave to the innkeeper, and said, 'Look after him, and on my way back I'll reimburse you for any extra expense you have had.'

Recognition can be a commodity which can be of value to us all. There are three recognitions:

R1   **Self:**   recognition of one's self;
R2   **Others:**   recognition of the selves of others;
R3   **System:**   recognition of the selves of systems.

If we treat recognition as a commodity, then it can be earned, traded and invested in, as are other commodities.

R1 – Self-recognition

Recognition of one's self is a legitimate recognition of the fact of one's existence, and a creative interest in the quality of one's existence and the preservation of one's existence.

Each person recognises the unique view that he or she has of situations, the unique way in which he or she selects and arranges information according to his or her unique experience

Self–recognition includes the right and willingness to change the way we look at things, to seek fresh and better arrangements of information, to build a better individual world in which we can live.

R2 – Other-recognition

Valuing recognition of one's self automatically carries with it value for the recognition of the selves of others. We recognise their reciprocal rights; their right to a unique view of situations, their right to the way they select and arrange information according to their unique experience; their right to live in their own worlds, as we live in ours.

Recognition of others includes the right and willingness to help them change the way they look at things, to help them see fresh and better arrangements of information, to help them build better individual worlds in which they can live – better, of course, in THEIR own view.

This is not merely the imposition of our view with the claim that since our view is 'right' for us, then it should also be 'right' for them. Recognition of others is the valuing and appreciation of plurality – a variety of opinions. Live and let live.

R3 - System recognition

Recognition of the system means realising that, on balance, if we are all to enjoy the maximum recognition as individuals, give goes along with take.

System recognition means understanding the paradox of structure and freedom. It is only with the structure of the bridge that we enjoy the freedom to cross the ravine. This paradox also means the freedom of productivity that comes with an electronic structure like the Internet; the freedom of a higher income that comes with the structure of acquiring new and more useful skills and strategies; the freedom of competence, confidence, and performance that comes with the structure of discipline, practice, and repetition.

Recognition of systems makes possible recognition of others, which in turn multiplies the recognition we can enjoy for ourselves.

Example:

Imagine there are ten people in a spaceship hurtling through space:

R1 First, if every individual passenger decides to recognise himself or herself, then each can enjoy the recognition of one person – his or her own self;

R2 Second, if every individual passenger decides to give recognition to the other passengers, each can enjoy the recognition of ten people – his or her own PLUS that of nine others;

R3 Third, this spaceship is really a classic social system; if each passenger decides to recognise the system then the system can continue to provide safety, progress, happiness, co–operation, and a feeling of self–importance or self–worth for all on board.

Planet Earth is such a spaceship.

Royal recognition

When it comes to understanding the concept of recognition a fine example is the Prince of Wales. The Prince, with a thousand years of tradition behind him, has emerged as one of the authentic leaders of the New Millennium.

Quite apart from those aspects of his life that so occupy the attention of the gossip media, the Prince has much more to offer us. He is a strong believer in the concept of training, practising and personal development; he has trained and served in the Royal Navy and is also well–known for his involvement in activities like steeplechasing, diving, parachuting and polo.

In addition, Anthony Holden in his book *Charles* lists his interests as Carl Jung, United World Colleges, organic farming, alternative medicine, architecture with a human scale, urban regeneration, youth development and wildlife (both animal and plant); writing that they are all:

'Pieces of a giant jigsaw which fits together as a cohesive world view. Between them they amount to a princely Bill of Human Rights based on Charles' belief in the innate qualities of the individual, his right to live in conditions in which he can take pride as part of a caring, prejudice-free community which functions smoothly and effectively'.

Recognition for Self

Prince Charles meets many people in centres of urban squalor. He works to encourage people to demand a say in what happens to them by stressing the importance and the effectiveness of self–help. He stresses, as fundamental to hi own belief system, the rights of the individual. He seeks to empower people to lead their own lives the way they consider best for themselves. The Prince of Wales' Trust has created jobs for over 40,000 young people through supporting viable new business start-ups by the under-30s. It is the most successful 'business angel' in Britain.

Recognition for others

The Prince also promotes the vital need for INTERDEPENDENCE. In this respect, his mentor Sir Laurens van der Post, adventurer and philosopher, had a great impact on Charles. Sir Laurens had a deep respect for the bushmen of Southern Africa who live in total harmony with the Kalahari Desert. The bushmen's spiritual beliefs are based on a balance of the individual with nature, with the village and the tribe – a balance of wholeness and interdependence.

In 1987 Sir Laurens took Prince Charles to commune together with his bushman friends and the Prince developed a love for the bushmen and for the wilderness and remoteness of their landscapes.

In Sydney, during Australia's 1988 bi–centennial celebrations, the Prince emphasised his support for Aboriginal land rights. When Australian actor Jack Thompson commented that after 200 years Australians are just now finding out what Aborigines have known for 40,000 years, the Prince interrupted him with, 'Those are my sentiments entirely'.

Recognition for the system

Charles often leads the way when it comes to speaking up against the crazy, suicidal disrespect to the life systems of our planet – the air, the water, the land and bio–diversity. In London in 1989, at a conference on CFCs (chlorofluorocarbons) the Prince insisted to delegates on the need for their complete elimination and charged governments with an urgent agenda to intervene.

Against the pollution of the ocean systems and the desertification of the rainforests and their species, the Prince spoke strongly, 'If we can stop the sky turning into a microwave oven we will still face the prospect of living in a garbage dump'.

On balance

Commenting on the personal challenge of his own unique position of great wealth and title, he said:

'I may have everything I need materially but there are other difficulties. One worries a great deal about one's responsibilities and everything else, trying to do the right thing, to have as balanced an approach as possible'.

Secret revolution

Commenting in *Millennium* on the Prince' role as a world leader of the New Age, Francis Kinsman writes:

'His emphasis on closeness to the earth and communion with the plant kingdom has given him a hard row to hoe with the media – 'A loon again!' sneered one tabloid headline.

But the reality is that the public is beginning to listen to the marching songs of the Prince's secret revolution. An appropriate quotation is one from Machiavelli's The Prince: 'There is nothing more difficult to take in hand, more perilous to conduct or more uncertain in its success than to take the lead in the introduction of a new order of things'. The planet is incredibly lucky to have Prince Charles and he deserves all the support and love that we can muster'.

22

HUMOUR

Q. How many Quantum physicists does it take to change a light bulb?
A. Into what?

HUMOUR INVOLVES THE appreciation of oddness. In humour there is the willingness to enjoy seeing the OTHER SIDE of things, the willingness to see fresh points of view, to see them and appreciate them without necessarily feeling the need to adopt them as one's own. Oscar Wilde suggested:

'Selfishness is not living as one wishes to live; it is asking others to live as one wishes to live. Selfishness always aims at uniformity of type. Unselfishness recognises infinite variety of type as a delightful thing, accepts it, acquiesces in it, enjoys it.'.

Stars and conformists

Humour (with u or without u) includes flexibility in the way we can look at information, the humour of creativity, and the humour of insight. Humour means seeing things in a different way. Appreciating the value of differences. Not just trying to make everything conform, not trying to force star–shaped pegs into square holes.

To do this, we have to cut off the pointy bits of the star and often, by doing this, we lose the biggest added-value that the star shape has to offer. While conforming has its value, starring has its added–value. You'll remember we discussed earlier that the 'habit of adding value' is what Quality is all about.

Humour is clever

Humour also embraces exploration and experiment and the willingness to create 'mistakes' and to be surprised. It also encompasses the ability to enjoy oneself, as well as humility. Humour allows freedom from arrogance, self–righteousness, hypocrisy, and false morality.

Humour is also freedom from self–bullying and the bullying of others. There's the humour of wisdom, the humour of balance and tolerance, the humour of plurality. The enjoyment of surprise, chance and variety. The good mood, the sound of laughter, good humour and good health.

Surprise is human

Humour involves the appreciation of surprise. That's why it is said that God mustn't have a sense of humour. The argument goes that if we define a God as omniscient (knows everything) then that God cannot be surprised. So, He/She cannot have a sense of humour. Whether or not this is true, God knows! What is true is that we're not gods, we're not know–it–alls. We are humans and we are most human when we are surprised.

For this reason, one of my TV favourites has always been those vignettes from Candid Camera. I've never failed to laugh heartily and never failed to shed a tear at the wonderful mix of cleverness, pathos, surprise and laughter.

Humour is serious

In 1918, George Meredith, literary critic, wrote in An Essay on Comedy that the 'Comic Spirit' is like a social guardian angel, there to help us whenever men:

'...wax out of proportion, overblown, affected, pretentious, bombastical hypocritical, pedantic; whenever it sees them self–deceived or hood–winked, given to run riot, planning shortsightedly, plotting dementedly.'

D.H. Munro in his *Argument of Laughter* (1951) says that delight in what is new and fresh and a desire to escape from boredom and monotony are important aspects of what is meant by a sense of humour. Arthur Koestler in *The Act of Creation* (1964) compares the creative insights of humour to be similar to the insights of poetry and science. 'The logical pattern of the creative process is the same in all three cases', says Koestler and that laughter is what follows when two incompatible or incongruous frames of reference are joined.

Examples:

He was an old lion–killer. The trouble was there were no more old lions left to kill, so he started killing young lions with a club. The trouble was there were 50 of them in the club.

Father Cannibal: Sorry I'm late, have I missed dinner? Mother Cannibal: Yes dear, everybody's eaten.

A prisoner is playing cards with his guards.On discovering that he's been cheating, they kick him out of jail.

Cognitive scientists like Piaget and Chomsky pay a lot of attention to the subject of humour and their findings are contributing both to our understanding of human language and human behaviour. As humour is so strongly a human phenomenon, the more we understand about it the more we understand things like CONTRADICTIONS and PARADOXES and human thinking in general.

Recently, interest in humour is developing among mathematicians who see connections between pure mathematics and catastrophe theory and the patterns of humour. An account of this is presented in John Allen Paulos' *Mathematics and Humour* (1980). And also, in physics and science, the similarities between the structure of humour and the structure of scientific breakthroughs has also been observed (see Thomas Kuhn in *Structure of Scientific Revolutions*, 1970).

The humour of change

Sometimes things change. They say the only thing that doesn't change is change itself. Change can be sudden and cataclysmic, like the Turkish earthquake, or slow and unnoticeable like a friend's weight–loss program. But change is change and, sometimes, things may never be the same again.

When I think of change in this way I'm often reminded of the TWTTIN phrase – That Was Then... This Is Now! – and of the humour that often accompanies this kind of change in circumstances.

The scientist's dogs

About ten years ago in Pasadena, California, I was having lunch with a couple of scientists. One was Paul MacCready who invented the Gossamer Albatross which won the prize for the first man–powered flight across the English Channel. The other was Murray Gell–Man who won a Nobel Prize for his discovery of the quark.

We came to discuss the role that creativity plays in scientific discovery. This led to a discussion about sudden insights like the Aha! phenomenon and then, inevitably, to the subject of humour Murray Gell–Man began to laugh and then he told us his dog story

At that time, Murray had two Dobermans and an avocado pear

tree. One of the Dobermans liked to eat the avocados when they fell from the tree, the other Doberman didn't care for the avocados at all. Murray's problem was to stop the first dog from eating his avocados. He tried a number of things but to no avail. But being the scientist that he is, he didn't give up. Then he had an idea... Aha!

Murray sprinkled cayenne pepper on an avocado to see if the dog would still eat it, the dog wouldn't touch it. So, triumphantly, he then sprinkled cayenne pepper on all the avocados that had fallen on the ground to teach the dog a lesson that avocados are for humans who are smarter than dogs, anyway.

The change in circumstances worked, more or less. The avocado–eating dog never ate another avocado; however, the other dog now began to eat all the avocados. His addiction was to cayenne pepper! TWTTIN!

Productivity is fun

But, how is all this helpful to you, as a clever necktop user, in a practical way, today?

Productivity! Whether you're in the factory, at school, at home, in sport, in the laboratory or on the stock market, the structure of humour is identical to the structure of quantum leaps, paradigm shifts, changes of mind, CVS-TO-BVS, innovation and risk–taking, with their subsequent rise in productivity.

Above all, the Clever Company must have a sense of humour. It must have a culture that encourages surprise, experimentation, learning and the continual search for a BVS. This is what is meant by QRH, the balance between the virtues of Quality, Recognition and Humour.

If a company cannot learn to escape from its own experience then it's stuck with it. There's either moving ahead or falling behind. Moving ahead with leaps of productivity is fun to do. Falling behind, failing and laying–off people is no fun at all.

Cognetics style

How would one describe the style of a clever brainuser? ... QRH.

How would one describe the environment of a clever family? ... QRH.

How would one describe the culture of a clever company? ... QRH.

How would one describe the policies of a clever country? ... QRH.

QRH Styleware is another mind tool if it becomes a habit of thinking, that will help you develop your necktop to its fuller potential.

Oh! and by the way, PTV can't cope with QRH.

QRH QRH QRH QRH QRH
QRH QRH QRH QRH QRH
QRH QRH QRH QRH QRH
QRH QRH QRH QRH QRH
QRH QRH QRH QRH QRH
QRH QRH QRH QRH QRH
QRH QRH QRH QRH QRH
QRH QRH QRH QRH QRH
QRH QRH QRH QRH QRH
QRH QRH QRH QRH QRH
QRH QRH QRH QRH QRH
QRH QRH QRH QRH QRH
QRH QRH QRH QRH QRH
QRH QRH QRH QRH QRH
QRH QRH QRH QRH QRH
QRH QRH QRH QRH QRH
QRH QRH QRH QRH QRH

PRR Personal Trainer™

PRACTICE REPETITION REHEARSAL
PRACTICE REPETITION REHEARSAL
PRACTICE REPETITION REHEARSAL
PRACTICE REPETITION REHEARSAL
PRACTICE REPETITION REHEARSAL
PRACTICE REPETITION REHEARSAL
PRACTICE REPETITION REHEARSAL
PRACTICE REPETITION REHEARSAL
PRACTICE REPETITION REHEARSAL
PRACTICE REPETITION REHEARSAL
PRACTICE REPETITION REHEARSAL
PRACTICE REPETITION REHEARSAL
PRACTICE REPETITION REHEARSAL
PRACTICE REPETITION REHEARSAL
PRACTICE REPETITION REHEARSAL
PRACTICE REPETITION REHEARSAL
PRACTICE REPETITION REHEARSAL
PRACTICE REPETITION REHEARSAL

23

PRACTICE

'What's my secret? I never stop practising.'

Bruce Lee (Kung-fu movie star)

IN MY BUSINESS I often get asked in media interviews and seminars, questions like:'What is the ultimate strategy for success?' Everyone, understandably, wants a quick fix, a secret passage, a short–cut.

If there really is a short–cut. If there really is a secret passage. If there really is a genuine answer to such a question, I think it is what I have called PRR – which stands for Practice–Repetition–Rehearsal.

Many people are not aware of the fact that the original concept of 'self–help' and 'individual personal development' were invented by the early orders of knighthood.

The stirrup

It was the invention of the stirrup in the 9th century that led to the idea of the knight. Now a horseman was much surer in the saddle and so the cavalry charge against a wall of infantry became possible. This reduced infantry to the role of support troops and attention became focused on the horseman or cavalier or knicht (German) and his special individual training and personal development.

165

When one is a serious student of the history and strategies of training and personal development, one must study and learn the concepts and strategies of the orders of chivalry.

Training and service

The noble principles – of training and service – separated the orders of knighthood from their military predecessors. The notions of excellence and quality – of developing one's ideals and physical prowess through tournaments and practice and of offering one's service to others – became the original concepts of chivalry and knighthood. This gave chivalry its peculiar quality which has endured for 900 years.

The new age of chivalry

All the original crusading orders of knights have been extinct for 200 years since Napoleon drove the last of them out of Malta in 1798. But today we see a big return to the ideals of training and service. Perhaps we are now in the New Age of Chivalry!

People around the world are attending seminars, reading books, buying tapes, attending training courses, gyms and so on at a rate that would make the ancient knights green with envy. You, yourself, reading this self–help book, are one of them.

All of this goes to show that there is a big trend in Britain, the United States and around the world for people to help themselves and to help each other, as never before in history. And the bottom line is practice, practice, practice.

So, remember this: seminars don't work! Books don't work on any subject unless you practise! On the other hand, practice always works. Repetition always works. Rehearsals always work.

The ultimate strategy: PRR

There is no doubt whatsoever in my mind, that the ultimate strategy for success in any area is Practice–Repetition–Rehearsal – or PRR.

Jungle warfare

During the Vietnam War, the Jungle Training Centre at Canungra in Queensland was considered one of the best in the world. In jungle warfare, one of the things soldiers must learn is what to do in the event of an ambush.

Now, of course, an ambush really is the worst situation you could be in. It's totally unexpected and the natural patterns of behaviour are not useful.

Imagine that you are going along a jungle path, nearly back at base camp, tired, certain you are safe. Suddenly, you run into an AMBUSH!! Suppose the ambush is on your left. They're lucky, they have the element of surprise. You try not to get into that kind of situation, but what if you do?

Opposite Way

Well, first, what is the natural thing to do? Naturally you will tend to run the opposite way, but all that does is to keep you clearly in the line of fire. Actually, the best thing to do is to turn left to face them and walk straight into the ambush, because on the other side of the ambush lies safety (and you even get chance to have a go at the other guys).

So that's what military trainers teach: when a group runs into an ambush coming from the left, the lead man is supposed to yell 'AMBUSH LEFT!!' and then everyone is supposed to turn left and counter-attack. But, in a highly emotional situation like an ambush, it's difficult to do that just because someone yells out 'AMBUSH LEFT!!'

You know you're supposed to turn left and walk straight into it. You could probably pass a written exam in that right now. You could probably even teach it to somebody else... But to actually DO it yourself is another matter. There's a huge difference between knowing and doing.

Royal Australian Air Force

At one time, in the RAAF, I was taught to eject from a plane. Again, you don't want to have to eject from an airplane, but when it's necessary there is no other choice. There are much more modem systems now, but the way I was taught on the Maachi Jet was this: you just reach up and pull down two little yellow and black striped handles.

That's all you have to do! Everything else happens automatically. What that does is to detonate a bomb under your seat which explodes and pushes you through the canopy of the plane. Not very pleasant.

Of course it's the lesser of two evils. If something goes wrong and you get the command 'EJECT! EJECT! EJECT!', at that moment you simply reach up and do it. You don't wait to think, 'This can't be happening to me.' You have to eject immediately! You have to go first before the front seat pilot does because if he goes first, the explosion of his seat will kill you.

No, you don't have any time to think it over. You must know that when you get that command you ARE going to reach up and do what's called for. Again, it's simple to know but difficult to DO.

Knowing vs doing

It's another case where there's all the difference in the world between knowing and doing. Doing takes skill, and skill comes with training. With practice, practice, practice over and over again you can do it. Then, when something or someone triggers the pattern with the command, 'EJECT!!', it will trigger your being able to actually DO it.

Patterning your brain

In a patterning system, like your biological necktop, PRR is the ultimate strategy for building the deep executive patterns that you choose to override the weaker ones.

> 'The most successful people in the end are those whose success is the result of steady accretion. It is the one who carefully advances step by step, with his mind becoming wider and wider – progressively abler to grasp any theme or situation – persevering in what he knows to be practical, and concentrating his thoughts upon it, who is bound to succeed in the greatest degree.'
>
> **– Alexander Graham Bell**

PRR is like your own personal trainer. When you use the PRR necktop software you always improve. What new insights are you developing on the subject of PRR? Do you understand the strategic relationship between PRR and skill development? Think of an example of how you personally benefited from PRR in the past.

24

REPETITION

> 'Sow an act ... reap a habit;
> Sow a habit ... reap a character;
> Sow a character ... reap a destiny.'

DR ERIC BIENSTOCK was Managing Director of the School of Thinking in New York and his work, as a dear friend and close colleague, was critical in helping us to get 'thinking' into the US schools.

Eric wrote a book called *Thinking for Results* and the main point about his book was that thinking is not just a pie–in–the–sky activity for those who have nothing better to do. Rather, that thinking is the quickest and best way to get superior results. And we do want results!

Results as consequences

One meaning of 'result' is consequence or outcome of something. The reason we think and then do something is because our action has consequences and we have decided we want those consequences.

A baby cries because it knows its crying will bring the attention of a parent. Politicians makes promises because they want your vote. A young teenager starts to smoke cigarettes because he or she hopes, as a result, to look older, or perhaps to fit in with friends, or maybe just to assert a degree of independence from a parent's authority.

We know that all actions have consequences and so we can

170

manipulate our behaviour to try and achieve the satisfactory outcome, the result we want.

Results as scores

Another meaning of 'result' is a scoreline. It might be a quantity or a formula obtained by some calculations or a measurement. For example, we read in the paper: 'The result of yesterday's TV telethon for Help a Child was £13,563,892 and surpassed last year's result'.

A company's quarterly sales figures, the daily stock market results, the results of a Gallup Poll or of an election are all examples of the way we use results to keep score. Of course, the most obvious use of results for scoring is in sports. Football results, racing results, time scores, point scores, first place, last place, strokes, kicks, punches, penalties, metres, centimetres and photo finishes are different ways of measuring results, for keeping score.

How to get results

Someone once said that you cannot score until you know where the goal posts are. My late friend and mentor, Fred Herma (author with Earl Nightingale of *KISS: Keep It Simple, Salesman,* used to talk about setting objectives in order to reach them.

He once told me that for over 25 years he had been a student of psychology, philosophy, religions, motivation, training, etc., and that he'd had the opportunity of working with many leading teachers in the United States like Dale Carnegie, Earl Nightingale, Frank Bettger, and Dr Norman Vincent Peale.

He went on to say that if he were asked to boil it all down into one principle, it would be this:

'Find out what it is you want then do what is necessary to get it.'

Process, not results

Here now, we come to a kind of paradox in this discussion of results. Whenever we want results, it's better NOT to focus on them. Isn't this odd? Doesn't this seem a contradiction? What do we focus on if we don't focus on the results? The answer is this: focus on the PROCESS that leads to the results.

In business, for example, many sales managements have kept their salespeople at a low performance level because of their preoccupation with results. Their perceived need to get every sale, close every deal get the order, often distracts them from focusing on the process of selling, which is getting the customer's attention, keeping it and making the customer happy.

In fact, in business, focusing on the result and trying to close the sale, often to the annoyance of the customer, has given the whole selling profession such a poor reputation that many customers actually treat salespeople with a certain amount of suspicion... *caveat emptor!*

Process equals results

Whatever you do you will always get a result. Results, good or bad, wanted or unwanted, are simply the end product of a process in performance!

Results are what you get when you do certain things... with skill. Wanting results is not enough. Expecting results does not constitute management or leadership. All the goal–setting in the world is meaningless talk without ability and skill. If you practise the process, there is no mystery to the fact that you will automatically get results.

There is no mystery that jugglers can juggle. Anyone can learn to juggle three balls after about two hours of practising the process of juggling. Merely wanting to juggle three balls is not enough.

Exhortation is a waste of time. Saying to someone, 'You've got to do three balls!' is tiresome and never works. But getting them to juggle, practising the process of juggling always leads to results, every time, without fail.

Managing for results

No manager can ever manage results by managing results. The wise manager knows you get results by managing the activity that produces results. You manage the process. The process of getting results is to practise the skill that leads to results. If you increase practice of the skill, you increase the skill. When you increase the skill, you increase the results. There is no way you can fail.

In this book you've seen that cognetics is the skill of changing CVSs into BVSs, the skill of improving situations, and the skill of getting results. It is also a shift in attention from results to the process of getting results, with the addition of training (PRR – practice, repetition, rehearsal).

The secret

And now we come to the special secret of how to get results. This is the most clever trick you can learn from this book. Are you ready?

(Trumpet fanfare and big drum roll, please!) ... Da dah!

The trick is to always set TRAINING goals, not just result goals. PRR!

Set your training goals: 5 hours, 50 hours. Log your training hours, log your progress, log the development of your skill, just as a person at the gym logs his progress, or a pilot logs his flying hours.

No pressure. No tension. No need to suddenly be at the 500–hour level when you haven't had the opportunity to do even five hours. Just log your hours of training and move gradually from your CVS to a BVS. That becomes your new CVS and you gradually move to another BVS, which becomes your new CVS.

You search for a BVS, you gradually move towards it, and so on. Training, training, training. Practice, practice, practice. Log your hours, hours, hours. PRR. This is the short–cut to success. It's the only sure way. It never fails.

This is the cognetic spiral. The gradual, tension–free improvement of situations. The Japanese call this Kaizen and claim it's been a fundamental cultural cause for their success as a productive nation. Onwards and upwards, better and better, step by step with REPETITION. The secret is to measure your training hours and to enjoy the process. Then, the results will take care of themselves.

Results = training hours = results...

As you will have noticed by now (groan!) we've placed a lot of emphasis on PRR, on practice, repetition, rehearsal. The reason should be very clear. It's because we want results! And, in training, results come from hours of:

> REPETITION REPETITION REPETITION...

The secret

And, as we've already discussed, the secret to getting results is to not only set results goals but to also set process goals, that is, TRAINING GOALS. Don't just set a result goal like: I want to be able to juggle. You also need to set a training goal like: I want to practise juggling for 10 hours. How do you juggle? PRR x 10 hours.

SOT training survey

In 1983, in New York, the School of Thinking conducted a survey to find out the training hours needed to acquire a basic operating skill and confidence in that skill in the following areas.

We thank the Juillard School in New York and other experts who gave the following estimates:

SKILL	HOURS
Piano	450
Singing	900
Alto sax	600
Cello	900
Flute	1200
Violin	1900
Trumpet	300
Trombone	600
Guitar	150
Harmonica	50
Reading music	150
Kung Fu	600
Juggling	2

It was pointed out by the experts that these hours of training would not be enough to produce a virtuoso ability, but would give a very sound operating or performing ability of skill in these areas.

The same, of course, applies to your own development of the skills of cognetics. The more hours you practise the better the skill you acquire. The better the skill you acquire the better the results for your life – and it's results we want.

So, there you have it. Ultimately results come from hours of practising. More hours = more results.

What have been some of the results you have got from the time you have spent reading this book and thinking about your own CVS? What are some of the results you expect to get in the future?

If you use PRR as your personal trainer you are bound to succeed.

25

REHEARSAL

OCTOBER 19, 1986. Driving from Manhattan to upstate New York on that late autumn Sunday, I remember thinking, 'Well, this may be my last day alive but it certainly is a gorgeous one!' I was headed for New Paltz, orchard country, and wherever you looked there were trees all ablaze in the autumn colours of reds, ochres, browns, citruses and the bluest sky I could ever recall seeing. Or perhaps it was simply fear that had heightened my senses.

The AFF

On arriving at the farm, my friend and host Carl Zatz met me with a hearty welcome, telling me how pleased he was that I actually showed up. 'Since you're here, you should do an AFF!' says Carl and before I could ask what an AFF was he launched into the introductions to the group of about ten 'first–timers' waiting for the commencement of the morning's instruction. By lunchtime we had covered everything and the instructor said 'OK, you can all break for lunch now and wait for your turn. Uh... not you Michael, you're going to do an AFF!'

I was immediately escorted off by two new instructors who suddenly emerged; and, as I looked back at my classmates, a little startled, they waved at me with a blend of curiosity and relief as I was led away. I knew then, that I should have made much stronger inquiries as to the meaning of AFF.

'Well, you can forget everything you learned in this morning's class because you will be doing an AFF – Accelerated Free Fall. I'm

Brendan Kennedy, your Main Side Jumpmaster, and this is your Reserve Side Jumpmaster...' In the fearful apprehension that suddenly blocked out my senses, I never did catch the other fellow's name.

My understanding had always been that, for a first–time parachute jump, you went up to around 3000 feet, jumped, and a static–line opened your 'chute automatically as you left the plane. However, an AFF, as I was now being told, meant going up to 12,500 feet and jumping from the plane, free-falling for 50 seconds and then popping your own 'chute – all on the first jump. The two jumpmasters would also jump with me on either side... just in case.

The dilemma

It's difficult to describe adequately the lack of enthusiasm that I was now feeling for the whole idea of jumping. But since I felt I had committed myself to the AFF, I was even less enthusiastic about cancelling out. There were some background reasons as to why I felt this way but it's enough to say that I found myself deep in a dilemma. And I made the decision that the only way to go was... up.

The decision

This is exactly how I thought through the decision.

First, I'll complete the training they plan to give me. That may make me feel better as I'll understand what's involved. Second, I presume these guys (both qualified US Parachute Association Jumpmasters) know their job and if I follow meticulously everything they tell me, then I should be OK. Third, in addition to the training they give me, I will do ten more rehearsals of my own, before I go up.

The training took about two hours after which they said to wait for my turn. Mine would be the last jump of the day because of the extra height to 12,500 feet and they wanted to do all the others before me. It was 1430 and I would go up around 1700. So, I went behind the barn and started to rehearse the drill they had taught me, ten more times.

The rehearsals

The drill was called a Circle of Attention. It involved focusing one's attention around a circle which included the horizon, focused eye contact with the jumpmasters on either side of me, the altimeter for height, and the drill for popping the 'chute. During the 50 seconds of my free fall I was meant to do the sequence twice as a practice, and on the third time to actually pull the handle on the rip–cord and pop the 'chute. All in all, not a terribly difficult thing to do... in theory. The only distraction was that I would be hurtling to earth at maximum velocity and, for obvious reasons, needed to do it right the first time. So I rehearsed the sequence ten times. I did this quite deliberately as a practical application of the PRR strategy we have been talking about. I did these rehearsals knowing from military experience that they would make me very proficient at the drill and much more likely to be able to do it well even in the highly emotional situation of my free fall.

The plane

After kitting up in the suit and parachute we boarded the plane. I sat on a bench on the left side of the plane opposite the special jump door on the right side. My two jumpmasters sat, very close to me, on either side. They were very hyped up and there was a great deal of 'Let's go do it!' and 'You look great, Mike.' Presumably this was to keep my spirits up, keep me occupied and stop me from pulling out, something that I would have very much liked to have done if the cost to my self–esteem hadn't been so prohibitive.

The omission

Eventually the plane reached the final circuit and levelled off at 12,500 feet. They opened the jump door and it seemed the whole side came off the plane. Now the sound of the cold air rushing by was roaring in my ears, cranking up the fear threshold; and as I peered out, the earth seemed just like a map. It was really, really high. You couldn't make out cars or houses, just the geometric shapes of the fields and the long silver snake of a river reflecting the rays of the setting sun.

Then the Main Jumpmaster said something that really threw me. Something that I hadn't rehearsed and something that sent an ice cold wave of panic throughout my body. He said, 'Get into position!' This entailed getting up off the bench, moving across to the other side of the aircraft and sitting on the edge of the plane with my legs outside the door, ready to jump. If I could have spoken at all, I would have said no – but the terror that gripped me was overwhelming. I knew I could jump, but the thought of *falling out accidentally* while getting into position really got to me – I hadn't rehearsed getting into position and that was what scared me the most. I only hoped I was not showing the anxiety I felt and tried to look reasonably cool.

The exit

Somehow I managed to get into position. Now I was sitting with legs dangling, 12,500 feet above the earth, cold air rushing past, about to jump out of a perfectly good airplane... I was so cross with myself for putting myself in such a unnecessary position, but the time had come. The main jumpmaster, now sitting tightly to my left, looked at me for positive eye contact. The man on my right then did the same. With a thumbs up signal we began the drill: lean forward, lean back... then forward again and out of the plane.

Free fall

I lost it for the first few seconds. The sheer quantity of new information being presented to me made me brown out. But then I snapped to again and continued the drill: check the horizon... now, positive eye contact with the jumpmaster on my left. Wow! Look at his face. His skin is flapping and rippling just like the astronauts. I suppose mine must be doing the same. He looks me right in the eye and acknowledges my consciousness with a grin and a friendly thumbs up sign. Drill: I then do the same with the man on my right. He makes me feel good with a firm acknowledgment that I'm OK and doing fine... check the altimeter – 10,000 feet – and then, repeat the drill, just like I rehearsed it.

Well, I just can't adequately explain the thrill that came with knowing that I was flying through the air like a bird, that everything was going just as planned, that I was in control and... no fear. And it was exquisite. The sun was setting to my left and the colours were vibrating in their atmospheric intensity. Ultra blues and pinks and shafts of solar lasers streaking here and there.

As I continued the drills the sheer ecstasy of flight became a euphoric high that bathed my whole being, replacing the cold panic that had been there only seconds ago. After three–quarters of a minute of free flight and approaching 5,000 feet it was time to pop my 'chute and break from formation with my 'guardian angels'. I found the steel handle of the rip–cord with my right hand as I balanced out by holding my left hand straight ahead. I pulled the handle. Whoosh! Everything suddenly changed. Not flying... hanging. Not fast... slow. Not watched... alone. And now I could see what I'd done. Wow!... I'd really done it and I was very pleased with myself. Now, the radio on my shoulder strap began to crackle. The ground controller began to give the instructions for me to fly the 'chute towards the landing zone.

The grin

The next few minutes consisted of left turns and right turns and 180s as I manipulated the controls of the 'chute. Finally, pulling both hands down and into a stall for the landing. I landed fine on both feet and it was all over. As my jumpmasters and others ran towards me, yelling and whooping and taking photographs, I began to feel myself grin and grin and grin and grin. Whether the grin lasted five days or only four is a detail which wasn't officially recorded. What was recorded in my

USPA Log Book was a rating of 'Excellent' and a recommendation to the next jump level. Thanks to the strategy of *ten* rehearsals!

PRR personal trainer: planning your own rehearsal

There must be something coming up for you soon that's really important for you to try and get an excellent result for yourself. Here's a chance for you to use PRR to plan a rehearsal and increase your chances of getting the result you want.

- WHAT: What is the situation that you'd like to rehearse?
- WHY: Why is this important to you?
- WHEN: When will it happen'
- WHO: Who else, if anyone, should be involved?
- HOW: How do you plan to do your rehearsal? How many times will you rehearse?
- WHERE: Where is a good place for you to rehearse?

PRR PRR PRR PRR PRR PRR
PRR PRR PRR PRR PRR PRR
PRR PRR PRR PRR PRR PRR
PRR PRR PRR PRR PRR PRR
PRR PRR PRR PRR PRR PRR
PRR PRR PRR PRR PRR PRR
PRR PRR PRR PRR PRR PRR
PRR PRR PRR PRR PRR PRR
PRR PRR PRR PRR PRR PRR
PRR PRR PRR PRR PRR PRR
PRR PRR PRR PRR PRR PRR
PRR PRR PRR PRR PRR PRR
PRR PRR PRR PRR PRR PRR
PRR PRR PRR PRR PRR PRR
PRR PRR PRR PRR PRR PRR
PRR PRR PRR PRR PRR PRR
PRR PRR PRR PRR PRR PRR

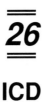

26

ICD

'Wealth is the product of an individual's capacity to think.'
– Ayn **Rand**

'Think and grow rich'
– Napoleon **Hill**

WHO ARE YOU? Are you a propeller–head, a scientist, working mother, a researcher, an academic, an engineer or maybe a salesperson or an actor? Perhaps you're in business or still at school or an undergraduate? Are you retired, politician, in the media, the military or a member of a religious order? Are you a neuro–surgeon or perhaps a croupier in a casino?

The boardroom factor

The point is: whoever you are, whatever you are doing, wherever you live in today's world, your life, your options and your future is being determined – today, tomorrow and ever day – in one unique environment... the boardroom. More than ever before in history, decisions that are being made in the boardrooms of multi–national corporations today are producing the world you will live in tomorrow.

Political systems are becoming obsolete. War, an extension of politics, is also becoming less viable. Today's world is being powered more by profit than by dogma. In the 21st century, more battles will be fought in boardrooms than on all the battlefields of human history.

Whether this is better or worse remains to be seen but it is a fact that needs to be understood. As always, if you don't do your own thinking others will do it for you.

So what does all this mean to you? How do you fit in? Where do you get to have an input? What can you do? What do you need to know? What skills do you need to develop? Let's start at the top...

Business maps

How does a Chief Executive Officer (CEO) make a strategic business decision?

How does an executive form an opinion on the balance between a return on an allocation of resources and the potential risk involved?

How do bankers or investors decide to invest their capital and how do they weigh up the balance between the hoped for Return On Investment (ROI) and the possible loss of their capital?

How do they 'see' a business? On what basis is their 'perception' of the business formed? How do they get a map of a business?

Medieval measurement

Amazingly, most of today's investment and business decisions are still based on an invention that has not been updated for over 500 years!

In Venice in 1494, Fra Luca Pacioli invented double–entry bookkeeping and published the world's first textbook on accounting principles and practice. Ever since, this has been the basis of investment decisions. Double–entry bookkeeping showed a map of how money and goods flow through a business.

This allowed investors and businesspeople to 'see' a business, evaluate risk and return and then form an opinion on whether or not to make an investment.

In those days, even on through the industrial revolution, business consisted of *things*. Things are tangibles like property, buildings, inventories, cash in the bank and so on. So the double–entry bookkeeping system seemed like a useful way of organising one's view of the ebb and flow of these tangibles, and one simply accepted this way of looking at things and then went on to make one's investment decision.

That was then, this is now

Since the knowledge and information revolutions, it's hard to imagine how young businesspeople could be misled more than to be given the impression that this is what today's businesses are still made up of – tangibles. Yet we find that in business colleges and MBA programmes around the world the medieval measurement, the 'double–entry' view of a business, is still being taught as though it were writ on tablets of stone.

In the 1990s we have computers that can do around 4 billion computations a second, yet we are still using pre–Newtonian mechanics to make our business decisions. In the next few years, this will have to change.

Knowledge–based companies

In knowledge-based companies, what does the traditional accounting system capture? Hardly anything.

The old accounting system is blind to knowledge-based assets and is often limited to just considering fixed asset values, labour and material costs. It cannot, for instance, measure the ability to adapt to change, other than in terms of worthless historical data. In today's fastest-growing, most market–responsive businesses, however, the cost components of many products are intellectual capital like R&D and customer-service.

As clever companies increasingly recognise their intellectual assets, they will increasingly direct their attention to developing those assets. When it comes to productivity, two heads are always better than one and that means networking intranets, extranets and the Internet.

In a recent edition of Arthur Andersen's *Outlook* magazine, partner Glover Ferguson of the firm's Centre for Strategic Research in Chicago writes:

'We are now witnessing, in today's world of technology-enhanced commerce, the emergence of a rich star – in this case a number: $3.5 trillion. That's the amount describing the enormous profits waiting for businesses along the universal network known as the 'information highway'. Perhaps at no time has technology dominated the news as it has of late. Major organisations are jockeying for positions at the cash flowpoints on the universal network, and their mergers and other initiatives have moved the business page to the front page.

'Far–seeing enterprises must develop computing and communications applications further up in their business processes, not just at the consumer interface. That's where the gold will be found. Organisations that recognise the magnitude of the coming changes and act now to rethink their basic processes, accessing the power of new technological capabilities, will move so far ahead so quickly that they will dominate their respective industries within IO years.'

Intellectual capital (IC)

These 'far–seeing enterprises' will be exploiting, managing and measuring the primary ingredient of their economic performance, their intellectual capital or IC as it is now being called. The intangible IC assets of information, knowledge and skill will be formalised, captured and leveraged to produce higher–valued assets, higher performance and a more profitable enterprise.

Also, hi–tech manufacturing companies of today and tomorrow will derive most of their 'value-added' from knowledge and skill. This will have to be accountable. Those businesses that are not accounting for their IC assets will be under-valued and left behind. Those that do will more than double their assets and move ahead.

ICD and investing in people

TQM was the buzzword of the nineties – Total Quality Management. The buzzword for the next decade, replacing, TQM, is ICD – Intellectual Capital Development.

In business, people are now becoming more important than money. IC is becoming the most valuable asset of many corporations. IC accounting is how a modern business gets a more accurate view of its people assets when knowledge is its chief resource.

Suppose you are an investor. You can form a more useful, realistic perception of companies like Microsoft by accounting for their 'soft' IC assets than you can by merely accounting for their 'hard' assets like their office buildings, cash and equipment.

- FACT: The value of the tangible (money) assets on today's balance sheet is exceeded many times by the value of the IC (people) assets of the enterprise.

- FACT: The intellectual capital of the enterprise is the raw material from which all financial results are derived.

- FACT: The intellectual capital owned by the enterprise can be measured, managed and developed along with the financial capital and tangible assets currently recorded on the balance sheet of the enterprise.

ICD and reward

A simple way to develop intellectual capital is to use the power of reward. It is well known in business that most people's productivity takes a quantum leap when they are rewarded in some way. Trainers know that you train a horse by rewarding the desired behaviours, even with just a cube of sugar.

A reward need not always be a lump of sugar but even a single lump of sugar is far better than nothing at all. A reward is anything that is perceived as such by the person being rewarded. It may be a wink or a smile. A pat or a handshake. It may be a kookaburra stamp on a workbook or an afternoon off work. A round of applause, a special plaque, a ribbon, a medal a title, or even a kingdom may be a reward for many people. A reward may be for one's own self, for another, or for the system.

For centuries, in addition to gold and land, many have used honours, titles and rank as rewards especially in the field of military training, battle experience and chivalry. When one risks death, one risks the very annihilation of one's own self. To do this one needs a very potent reward.

For some, great wealth is the ultimate reward. For others, recognition by one's peers has great value. Yet others found the promise of an immortal self was the most irresistible reward of all, and one for which death seemed a fair price to pay.

Rewarding and results

Nothing gets better results than rewarding. As a manager, what you reward is what you get. Whatever gets rewarded, gets done! In business, if you reward your customers with better service than your competitor, your customers will reward you with their business.

In personal relationships, many people prefer partners who reward them to those who do not. Most children prefer adults who reward them. Most senior executives work harder for rewards, than they do for food and shelter.

In science, Skinner, Pavlov, Maslow, James, Gallup and others have demonstrated, in hundreds of experiments, the productive power of reward. If you want results, give rewards. If you want ten times better results, give ten times more rewards. Better is not always quantity; but if profits increase, why not share them?

Reward power

As with most instruments of power there are two sides to the power of reward: giving and receiving.

Some people have difficulty with receiving a reward for their efforts or they may be embarrassed at the prospect of receiving special recognition. I have noticed this more in Australia than in the US and it may have something to do with the common phenomenon known as the Tall Poppy Syndrome, which is this habit some Lazy Critics have of 'knocking' people over who stick their head above the crowd.

Tall Poppies

The lazy critics' pastime of belittling the efforts of others must surely affect our productivity. If we are uncomfortable with rewarding other people's attempts at cleverness then we cannot expect others to have a go. This PTV syndrome is an unwanted hindrance to the development of our intellectual capital and our goal of putting British industry on the world map again.

For, if we are insecure about our peers' reaction to our own attempts at cleverness then we cannot really be expected to try too often. Is this what we want? Isn't is better to be a tall poppy than a little weed?

What reward will you give yourself for finishing this book?

Summary of PART TWO

SDNT CVSTOBVS QRH PRF
SDNT CVSTOBVS QRH PRF
SDNT CVSTOBVS QRH PRF
SDNT CVSTOBVS QRH PRF
SDNT CVSTOBVS QRH PRF
SDNT CVSTOBVS QRH PRF
SDNT CVSTOBVS QRH PRF
SDNT CVSTOBVS QRH PRF
SDNT CVSTOBVS QRH PRF
SDNT CVSTOBVS QRH PRF
SDNT CVSTOBVS QRH PRF
SDNT CVSTOBVS QRH PRF
SDNT CVSTOBVS QRH PRF
SDNT CVSTOBVS QRH PRF
SDNT CVSTOBVS QRH PRF

The Author

Michael Hewitt-Gleeson is the Founder and Principal of the School of Thinking.

The School of Thinking (SOT) teaches 'thinking as a skill'. SOT lessons have already reached over 50 million people worldwide. Based on the Internet, SOT is now the largest school in the world and has received the coveted 'top 5per cent of the Web' award of all Internet sites. SOT provides daily interactive training in thinking and intellectual capital development. Anyone. Anytime. Anyplace.

Dr Hewitt–Gleeson is a cognitive scientist whose research has been in designing human thinking strategies and what he calls *Software for Your Brain*, the title of his best–selling book. He is the originator of NewSell, a break–away approach to selling which also became a best–selling book.

He was recognised by the US Government as 'a national asset' for introducing into the United States in 1979, the first nationwide programme ever to teach thinking as a skill to business, education and public markets.

He has been invited to lecture in many countries, including the UK.

His ideas have been sought by organisations such as: IBM, General Electric, Borg–Warner, General Motors, Mobil, the United Nations, the United States Army, USMC, the US State Department, The White House, NASA, the Royal Australian Air Force, Saudia Airlines, Coca-Cola, SmithKline Beecham, BMW, Scania, Hewlett–Packard, JLW, The Actors Institute (New York), The Australian Institute of Management, The University of Melbourne, Royal Melbourne Institute of Technology, McLuhan & Davies (Toronto), The Gallup Poll (Princeton), the Cognitive Research Trust (Cambridge UK), the Young Presidents' Organisation (Houston), The Executive Connection (TEC) and others.

To contact the author

If you wish to discuss lectures, seminars, training or assistance in developing your organisation's intellectual capital, send your e-mail to <mhg@sot.com.au>.

To visit the School of Thinking

If you wish to visit the School of Thinking or become a member and get involved in the training and activities of SOT the home page is at <www.sot.com.au>.